70 PLAY Activities

For Better Thinking, Self-Regulation, Learning and Behavior

Lynne Kenney, PsyD

with Rebecca Comizio, MA, MA-Ed, NCSP

Published by
PESI Publishing & Media
PESI, Inc
3839 White Ave
Eau Claire, WI 54703

Cover: Amy Rubenzer
Editing: Bookmasters
Layout: Bookmasters & Amy Rubenzer
Illustration: Megan Garcia

Printed in the United States of America

ISBN: 9781683730194

PESI
Publishing
& Media
www.pesipublishing.com

Dedications

In my earliest years my mother taught me how to read and play with enthusiasm. From picture books to tea parties, creativity and imagination were celebrated in our family. This book is dedicated to my mother, for her focus on loving communication, attachment and play and to my father, brothers, husband, and our children for their commitment to education, family and community. We live to 'lift one another up.' I hope this book inspires you to build confidence and competence with kindness and caring, in your students, clients and family.

Lynne Kenney, PsyD

This work is dedicated to my four children whose growth and learning fill my life with inspiration and to my husband whose love, support and partnership fills my heart with purpose.

Rebecca Comizio, MA, MA-Ed, NCSP

About the Authors

Lynne Kenney, PsyD, is a Harvard-trained psychologist, the mother of two teens, an international educator, and a pediatric psychologist in Scottsdale, Arizona. Dr. Kenney is co-author with Wendy Young of *Bloom: 50 things to say, think and do with anxious, angry and over-the-top-kids* and author of *The Family Coach Method.* Her most recent digital book *Musical Thinking: Steps to Teaching Children How They Think* introduces her direct instruction method to improve executive function skills.

Dr. Kenney has advanced fellowship training in forensic psychology and developmental pediatric psychology from Massachusetts General Hospital/Harvard Medical School and Harbor-UCLA/UCLA Medical School. In her Bloom BrainSmarts presentations to over 4000 clinicians, parents and teachers, Dr. Kenney integrates neuroscience, kinesiology and music research to enhance executive function, social-emotional and academic skills with motor movement. Dr. Lynne's cause-related program, Play Math, helps children ages 6-12 learn their math facts with playground balls and hula-hoops for better algebraic thinking. For more visit: www.lynnekenney.com.

Rebecca Comizio, MA, MA-Ed, NCSP, is the mother of four wonderful teenagers. She is a dedicated and driven, Nationally Certified School Psychologist working to utilize her education, training and life experience to positively affect the lives of children and families by advocating for students. Rebecca applies her studies of Education and Psychology to support the social-emotional and psychological needs of students in order that they become more able to succeed and flourish in academic settings. She thrives on continual learning and has earned a Bachelor of Science in Philosophy & English Education, from Central Connecticut State University, a Master's Degree in Philosophy & Education from Teachers College, Columbia University, and a Master's Degree and professional certificate in School Psychology from Iona College. Rebecca is currently working as School Psychologist and the Director of Social-Emotional Learning at the Stanwich School, a PreK-12th grade independent school in Connecticut.

Table of
Contents

Introduction

Play. It makes the world go 'round. We often hear "Play is the language of childhood." And it is. Children develop their cognitive, motor and learning skills through play beginning in the first few months of life. Playing within a safe, secure relationship helps children develop not only their developmental skills but also their sense of security, mastery, confidence and independence.

Play is the foundational activity that brings humanity together. Since the beginning of time, even before we humans spoke, we played. We played with sound, we played through nonverbal gestures and we played with movement in order to grow together as social beings (Lieberman, 2013).

When people learn that I am an educator in child brain development they often ask me, "What's the one thing I can do to help my child develop to his fullest potential?" Although there are many critical factors such as good quality nutrition (free of pesticides, herbicides and added hormones), emotional attunement and physical safety, once those "Top 3" are met, I suggest to parents that they get down on the floor and play with their children. "Play now, play later, play more."

Even in this digital era, one in which Dr. Hilda Kabali at the Einstein Medical Center in Philadelphia reported that 1 in 3 American children under age one have played with a tablet or smartphone, play remains at the heart of our cognitive, motor and social interactions.

This book, *70 Play Activities For Better Thinking, Self-Regulation, Learning and Behavior*, is all about play. How to play, when to play, where to play and with what to play. These activities grew out of our clinical and educational work with over 2000 children in the past 30 years. The activities in this book are created with the brain in mind. They are specifically designed to improve thinking, self-regulation and learning by applying neuroscience to clinical practice.

Let's Talk About You

If you are a clinician or teacher working with children who have difficulty with attention, concentration, distractibility, planning, organization, goal-setting, time management, task initiation, task completion, impulse control, mood management or inhibition you spend a good deal of your time helping children develop strategies to help them succeed. You hold team meetings, write IEP goals, perform task analysis and look for innovative ways to enhance children's skill sets.

There may be many times when you search online or in books for activities that will help you meet the needs and treatment goals of the children with whom you work. This book is designed to be that resource for you. It's the book you open when you are planning for the next session or series of sessions with a specific child, group of children or even an entire class.

I like to think of this book as an inspiring recipe box. Instead of seeing every activity as cast in stone, think of them as "jumping off points" for your own creativity. Change them around, improve them and use them to meet the practical considerations of your own office or classroom. Where we provide you with worksheets, words and activities, you are free to create your own. We encourage you to involve the children.

I have a little story about that. In our first two books, *The Family Coach Method* and *Bloom: 50 Things To Say, Think And Do With Anxious, Angry and Over-the-top Kids* with Wendy Young, we have a feelings identification and mood management activity called Anger Mountain. I have used this activity for at least 10 years, and children love it.

One day as I was using Anger Mountain, the child with whom I was playing said, "Hey, Dr. Lynne, Anger Mountain is upside down. You have the explosive moments at the top of the mountain but the area to write in is the smallest. Actually, the bigger parts of the mountain should be at the top, because my explosions are HUGE!" I told him he was absolutely correct and I went home that evening and remade Anger Mountain. I encourage you to do the same with the activities in this book. Make them as individualized and specific as you desire or as the children need.

Children Love to Teach

We also do another thing with the children with whom we work that I wish to mention at the outset. Sometimes I am working with a child and when I say, "Shall we act this out," or "Play this out," or "Make a game out of this," we often do. As an example, Sun Salutation was created by myself and two gifted children whom I saw for years. When the children change, improve or even create a completely new game, sometimes I say, for example, "Janie, that is so terrific, I can see how many children would be helped by this activity. Shall we name it, then when I help other children, you will know that you are helping in spirit as well." Many of the children with whom I work have seen many therapists. They have had substantial difficulties for a long time. When we take the time to say, "Hey this is such a great idea, we could help a lot of kids with this activity," the children often feel appreciated, honored and celebrated. Further, the children are taken out of the role of patient, one they have occupied, perhaps for too long, and they climb into the role of mentor, teacher and helper. This can be a rewarding experience for a child who has been working hard to develop new thinking, feeling and doing skills for many years.

That is really what it all comes down to. **When we play activities, such as the ones in this book, we hope the children experience a feeling of growth, competence and celebration for their hard-fought efforts. They deserve it!**

Where It All Began

When I reflect, I think this book started in 1972 on the playground of Hubbard Woods Elementary school where I discovered I was good at "Jacks." As a somewhat shy little girl, I was not at the top of the social hierarchy in elementary school. But that all changed one day when I beat a super popular third grader at Jacks. Ah, the power of games. All of a sudden I shot up to head honcho, lead Jacks player and future playologist.

Fast forward to 1984 when I was earning my master's degree in physical education at the University of Southern California. I know, not such a sexy degree. Now they call it kinesiology or neuroscience; that would have been cooler. But the 80s being what they were, big hair, Madonna and all, that was what I earned, a master's in PE with a specialization in sport psychology.

Well, I kind of lucked out because in 1984, the Olympics were held in Los Angeles. And we sport psychology types were called upon to conduct imagery work with some of the Olympic athletes. So, at 6 o'clock in the morning, I'd head out to the track, swim stadium or baseball field and walk nervous athletes through the mental game of imaging the ideal pole vault, the fastest race, the winning moment and the like. Imagery worked and that was just the beginning.

Through my valued relationship with The National Head Start Association in 2007, I was introduced to SparkePE.org. I took their early childhood training two-day course and observed that playing with balls, hula-hoops and polyspots truly engaged the bodies and minds of children. As a pediatric psychologist, I began to incorporate movement and play into my sessions with children who carried diagnoses of ADHD, anxiety and learning disabilities. As we played to develop better sustained attention, impulse control, problem-solving and self-regulation, it was apparent that we could really improve children's thinking, motor and self-regulation skills by integrating what we knew in pediatrics, occupational therapy, music therapy, art therapy and PE. Thus, the evolution of this book.

Enterprise Skills

While studying research on executive function, mindfulness and self-regulation skills, it has often struck me that the activities we do in our practices enhance Life Skills, but not only that. The skills we teach are a different kind of skill; they are almost "future skills."

I was having a difficult time finding the word that described the skills I thought we were building with children in our offices. I even asked a group of colleagues I once invited to my home to brainstorm for Marlaine Cover's Parenting 2.0 Leadership Initiative about the most essential ways in which education needs to evolve in order to better meet the needs of students in this era, "What are the skills of the future called?"

Then, one day, I was talking with parenting author Sue Atkins, from the United Kingdom, and she said, as she often does, "I have a colleague I wish to introduce you to." Her name was Lorraine Allman of Enterprising Child, a business skills learning program in England. And right then, like a lightning bolt from the sky, I knew "Yes, that is it! We are teaching children Enterprise Skills." The skills needed to be a successful social being in a time when interpersonal, problem-solving and thinking skills are needed to such a degree that one is competent enough to plan for, prepare for and succeed in jobs that have not been created, with technology that does not yet exist and in a social and academic world that will be very different for the next generation when compared with what it is today.

So when you read the activities in this book and I reference some of the specific, neuropsychologically-oriented skills each activity might be well-suited to improving, think Enterprise Skills, not only executive function and self-regulation. Remain broad minded, creative and flexible, then these activities will really help the children with whom you work because you will bring your "whole self" to the moment knowing that you are not simply meeting a treatment goal. You are helping a child to become healthy, happy, competent, whole and enterprising.

What This Book Is and What It Is Not

70 Play Activities **is a book written for clinicians, teachers and parents eager to introduce more interactive play into the lives of the children with whom they work and whom they love.** The tenor of this book is predicated on the Bloom collaborative philosophy Wendy Young and I wrote about in *Bloom: 50 Things To Say, Think and Do with Anxious, Angry and Over-The-Top Kids*. The Bloom mindset is what helps these activities be effective. Our interactions with children throughout *70 Play Activities* are kind, cooperative and caring. When we move from a punitive or corrective stance to one of partnering in problem-solving, respecting the authentic viewpoints and experiences of the children, and partnering with the children, learning and behavioral improvements evolve naturally. Thinking and self-regulation skills include the mind-body relationship, the impact of relational connections on learning and the relational context of growth and development. Improving thinking skills exists within relationships; this is where the growth takes place.

The activities in this book were mostly created with children as we played in our offices, in schools, on playgrounds, on tennis courts and more. We are super fortunate because, when I told Rebecca Comizio, a talented school psychologist in Connecticut, about *70 Play Activities*, she generously shared many of the executive function activities she uses weekly with children at The Stanwich School. The Musical Thinking sections were further inspired by Nacho Arimany, whom I met through my kind colleagues Alex Doman and Sheila Allen of Advanced Brain Technologies. My deepest gratitude to my creative colleagues, Megan Garcia, Wendy Young, Megan Hunter and to you, for continuing to help these activities adapt and evolve to suit the needs of a broad range of children in diverse settings worldwide.

Although the activities in this book are empirically informed, they are not evidence-based. The activities are a creative response to the current research in kinesiology, occupational therapy, cognitive science, physical therapy and speech language therapy. The activities are not a formal "brain training program." They are designed to augment current treatment protocols and educational programming. *70 Play Activities* provides the clinician, educator or parent with creative activities to enhance thinking, self-regulation and learning skills through play.

For programs that address a variety of brain functions such as auditory processing, working memory, attention, speech, language and more, you might wish to research PREP, Cogent, Bright Start, Cogmed, Lumosity, Bal-A-Vis-X, BrainWare Safari, The Listening Program, inTime, Meludia, Lindamood-Bell, MC2, neurofeedback, Tools of The Mind, The Eaton-Arrowsmith Program, Social Thinking, 360 Thinking and Zones of Regulation.

These programs vary as to research support. Some are clinical in nature; others have case study data such as The Listening Program, Bal-A-Vis-X, BrainWare Safari and MC2. Still others such as PREP, Cogent, Tools of the Mind, Activate, Cogmed and The Eaton-Arrowsmith Program have been subject to peer-reviewed scientific study. Research findings vary as to efficacy.

It is best to read and understand the research supporting any activity-based program you utilize. Some people whose work might interest you include Leonard Koziol, J. P. Das, Carl Haywood, Nacho Arimany, Alex Doman, Sheila Allen, Howard Eaton, Barbara Arrowsmith-Young, Stacey Shoecraft, Suzy Koontz, Jean Blaydes-Madigan, Ross Greene, Martin Fletcher, Judy Willis, Tosca Reno, Donna Wilson, Eric Jensen, David Nowell, Sarah Ward, Leah Kuypers, Adele Diamond, Ann Alexander, Michelle Garcia Winner, Anita Werner, Zolton Dienes, Lev Vygotsky, and Alexander Luria.

How to Use This Book

Throughout *70 Play Activities* there are many choices of activities. It's important to try to match the activity not only with the child's developmental level and skill set but also with their current level of scaffolded skills. In order to make every activity a pleasant and useful learning experience, it's important to consider the student's current level of learning ability.

Most of the activities are generally applicable to children ages 6 to 12, but we have worked with clients ages 4 to 72. Remember, all of these activities provide an opportunity for a valuable learning experience. **The activities are designed to be playful, fun, creative and flexible.**

Additionally, many of the activities are hands-on activities; we want the child to interact with you, with other children or their family members as they are doing these activities. And we want them to think in adaptive ways about how to change, modify, improve or personalize the activities so that they can enjoy them even further.

When a child has a choice in selecting or modifying their activities, their personal involvement increases, improving their motivation and their learning. Therefore, include the children as much as possible not only in the choice of activity but also in the application of the activity.

When a child moves from doing an activity to teaching another how to do it, cognitive functions such as successive processing, inhibition, narrative language, organization and planning are all utilized. So think, create, write, draw, play to your heart's content.

Many of the activities are written in a format similar to the SPARKPE curriculum. For these activities, you might wish to copy the page and use it like a lesson plan. Other activities are in a more narrative format or there might be a graphic for an activity with just a touch of editorial. Where appropriate, in some activities, we have written a few of the executive function skills we discuss with the children in the section called "skill sets." We do not overwhelm the children by naming all the skill sets, we simply choose one or two to talk about at a time, as we play the activity.

For every activity you are free and encouraged to adapt them to your child, client, students or setting. Further, I hope these activities will inspire you to create your own. Children love making up activities and doing so, by itself, is a great executive function development process.

> We have found that some exercises, particularly when they include movement, are easier to understand when you can see them. Therefore, we have made videos of many of the exercises. They can be found on Dr. Kenney's YouTube Channel http://bit.ly/Bloom4

Finally, we now know from brain research that a lot of learning and storing of information happens during rest. So we need to strike an appropriate balance between learning activities and calming activities, quiet learning activities and active learning activities, so that the children have moments of time between activities during which their brains and their bodies can quietly rest for optimal learning and behavioral change.

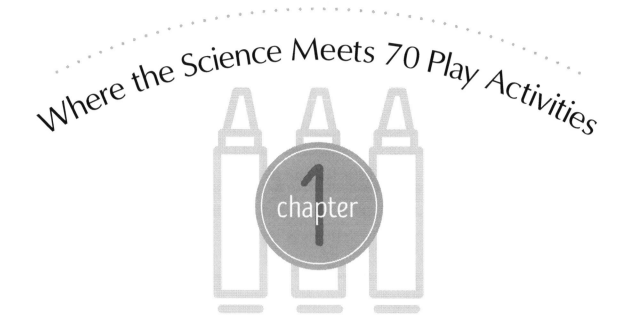

Where the Science Meets 70 Play Activities

chapter 1

If you have attended a professional training on executive function in the past 10 years, you have heard researchers and educators speak about executive function skills as cortical in nature – that is, residing in the frontal lobes of the brain. There are many studies on the role of the prefrontal cortex in the development and utilization of executive function skills.

Yet, in the past five years, advances in research, using technology such as functional magnetic resonance imaging and diffuse tensor imaging, have brought to light the relationship between the cortico-cerebellar, cortico-striatal and cortical-thalamic loops in relation to improvements in thinking skills and self-regulation. These loops are neural pathways that connect relevant parts of the brain for brain function and communication (Mathai & Smith, 2011). The role of the limbic system and cerebellum in thinking and self-regulation has become a central point of interest (Koziol & Budding, 2009; Koziol, 2014; Ito, 2011).

As Koziol (2014) reports, the cortico-basal ganglia and the cerebro-cerebellar circuitry systems are fundamental to cognitive and behavioral control. The basal ganglia anticipate and guide implicitly learned behaviors. The responses of the basal ganglia are central to the reward outcome systems within the brain. The cerebellar-cortical network anticipates and integrates information from the sensorimotor system, our initial feedback system within the brain. Behaviors are adapted and changed based on the feedback systems within the vertical integration. These vertically organized systems, operating together, represent the underpinnings of cognitive control. Cortical control is a whole brain response, not simply the response of one part of the brain. The brain works more like an orchestra than simply a section of instruments.

When we consider brain anatomy, we recognize the importance of the integration of the cortical and subcortical structures of the brain in learning and behavior. We need to keep front of mind that the higher level cognitive systems rest on the subcortical structures, including the limbic system and the cerebellum. Proper integration is needed for high-quality learning. As the phylogenetically older of the brain systems, the cerebellum precedes the prefrontal cortex, in the automaticity of learning and behavior. Both are stored in and mediated by the cerebellum. In fact, when we teach a new skill to a child, such as how to read simple phonics, at the point where that skill is so well known that it is automatized, the prefrontal cortex fires much less because less information needs to be processed by the cognitive control system. Further, working memory is less taxed when skills are automated, freeing up the prefrontal cortex to process more difficult scaffolded information. The layering of behavior and learning begins with automaticity. I observe that when large motor rhythm is well established before the introduction of a new behavioral or academic skill, the large motor rhythm exists as a platform on which the more highly scaffolded cognitive skills can rest.

I believe that two precursors to learning and behavioral change that will be further studied in the near future are rhythm and timing. While we often begin the discussion of reading with phonics and the conversation regarding numeracy with symbol-quantity match, I have seen in hundreds of children that when we begin teaching self-regulation, cognitive control, behavioral intention, reading and math with predictable and consistent motor rhythm and timing, the children's abilities to execute higher order behavioral and academic tasks improve exponentially. Why is this? Because motor rhythm and timing are precursors to behavioral and academic learning. Further, patterning which is a central element of learning, coincides with tempo, rhythm and timing in both reading and math (Center on the Developing Child, 2015).

Research now suggests that motor movement-based activities, rhythm and timing open the neural pathways in the cortico-striatal and cortico-cerebellar loops within the brain. These pathways enhance the connections and communication between the limbic, cerebellar and executive function systems. These neural pathways are central to brain organization and brain function as it relates to thinking, self-regulation and learning.

The relationship between gross motor skills, executive function, and academic achievement in children inspires clinicians to creatively incorporate art, music, movement, and play into their daily practice. Current research supports the budding relationship between movement and cognition in fostering executive function skills, self-regulation, and prosocial behavior. Yet the research is not so advanced as to study the complicated intersection of motor movement activities, cognitive control and learning. There is some research that studies:

- Exercise and cognition
- Physical activity and academic achievement
- Physical fitness and academic achievement
- Motor output timing and ADHD
- Motor output timing and grammar
- Computer exercises to improve memory
- Music, cognition and academic performance

We look forward to seeing more specific research on the role of gross motor movement, rhythm, and timing as the field of neuroscience grows.

In *70 Play Activities*, we use the basic component of Musical Thinking, rhythmic movement, as a foundational activity when we teach children new behavioral, self-regulation and academic skills. We then add cognition to the automated motor rhythm to enhance learning and behavior. We often increase the difficulty of the cognitive exercises in a step-wise manner, requiring a bit more of the child, as their experience and learned responses increase. As an example, after we introduce Musical Thinking, we may apply it to learning phonemes, graphemes, phonics, then whole words all the way up to complete sets of narrative instructions, such as "How to Organize Your Backpack." We have taught children how to maintain their alertness in class, raise their hands to answer a question in a more socially acceptable manner, walk in a line at school and more, using Musical Thinking.

Why Is Physical Activity so Important?

Curiously, the observed decrease in opportunities for movement and exercise in children over the past decade has coincided with an increasing body of literature that shows that motor development, movement and exercise facilitate thinking and learning.

In the "Shape of the Nation" report in 2012, it was noted that 46 states required mandatory physical education classes for at least some grades. Recently my colleague, Paul Rosengard, past Executive Director for SparkPE.org, informed me that only six states mandate PE in every grade. Although many of us never liked "dressing out," for PE, for many children their PE class is one of the primary opportunities they have to move within a school day. Although there is no federal mandate for PE classes in school, the U.S. Department of Health and Human Services Physical Activity Guidelines for Americans recommends that children and adolescents (ages 6–17) engage in 60 minutes or more of physical activity daily, including aerobic, muscle strengthening and bone strengthening exercises.

If you have ever used a pedometer, FITBIT® or app to track your daily exercise, you know that simply walking around your home or office, doing your daily chores or running your children between activities earns you anywhere from 800–3,000 steps per day, depending on how active you are. But when you add 45–60 minutes of aerobic exercise to your day, that often adds 3,000–5,000 to your total steps. Try it, you will see. You often hear that we need to take 10,000 steps per day for health benefits, and it is true there are research studies that show overall health improvements in several populations when one moves 10K steps per day, but even 7,000–8,000 per day is likely to improve your health.

Why do we need to get moving and even start counting? Because movement and exercise build your brain and body. When you move you increase the circulation of oxygen throughout your body, including your brain. Oxygen facilitates thinking. Exercise has been shown to improve blood circulation, reduce diabetes, improve heart health, lessen depression and reduce anxiety. Further, exercise may improve brain myelination, neural connections and neurotransmitter function.

Neurotrophins, such as brain-derived-neurotrophic-factor (BDNF), increase with moderate exercise, improving learning, concentration and memory (Griffin et al. 2011; Ratey, 2013). Glial cell-derived neurotrophic factor (GDNF) is currently being studied as well and appears to increase in the spinal cord with exercise, protecting the brain from cognitive declines associated with age (Budni, Bellettini-Santos, Mina, Garcez, & Zugno (2015).). Neurotrophic factors are secreted proteins that display an important role in synaptic and neuronal growth, pruning, myelination, differentiation, and survival of neuronal function.

Physical Activity, Academic Achievement and Cognitive Function

While there are several studies correlating improvement in adult cognition with exercise, relatively few studies have been conducted on children's cognition and exercise. Three review articles illustrate the variety of research findings: Sibley and Etnier 2003; Tomporowski, Davis, Miller & Naglieri, 2008; and Diamond, 2015.

The relationship between physical activity, academic achievement and cognitive function is generally studied in two broad categories: The benefits of physical activity, fitness or exercise on academic achievement and the impact of physical activity on cognition. The studies vary significantly in design, methodology and subject characteristics. Some studies look at the relationship between overall fitness and academic achievement. Other studies look at the relationship between exercise and cognitive function. For our purposes, achievement is usually measured by report cards, standardized testing or specific test scores. Cognitive function studies are usually more specific and examine aspects of executive function or cognitive control such as planning, working memory or inhibition, often using neuropsychological tests.

Here is a general summary of the findings to date:

- Physical fitness has been shown in many studies to have broad health benefits for children.
- A positive relationship between physical fitness and achievement has been observed in several studies.
- A positive relationship between physical fitness and some measures of cognition have been observed.
- General physical activity (resistance training, motor skills training, physical education interventions and aerobic training programs) and gains in cognitive function have been reported with low to moderately positive correlations. (Tomporowski et al., 2008; Diamond, 2015).
- Acute physical activity, meaning physical activity in close proximity to the achievement or cognitive measure event, has shown moderately positive correlations (Tomporowski, 2003a; Hillman et al., 2009).
- Physical activity that is paired with specific cognitive tasks shows some merit and is an area researchers have suggested needs more research.
- It is likely that "cognitive exercise" physical movement paired with increasingly complex cognitive demands impacts thinking, self-regulation and learning, specifically when children show initial deficits in related aspects of executive function before the intervention.

Sibley and Etnier (2003) conducted a meta-analysis of the research related to physical activity and cognition in children. At the time, there were only nine peer-reviewed studies using a true experimental design. After a review of 44 studies overall, the authors concluded that there is a positive relationship between physical activity and cognitive functioning in children. Further, they noted cautiously that there is some evidence that physical activity might cause cognitive improvements.

Tomporowski, Davis, Miller and Naglieri (2008) reviewed the research on children's intelligence, cognition and academic achievement and observed a broad range of findings. In general, physical activity was found to have a positive impact on learning in children. According to these authors, research findings suggest that systematic exercise programs may enhance the development of specific types of mental processing.

Researcher Charles Hillman at University of Illinois and his colleagues conducted a series of studies on the relationships between aerobic exercise, cognition and academic achievement. In one study, they examined the relationship between physical fitness and academic achievement in third to fifth graders and observed a correlation between math and reading scores and physical fitness (Castelli et al., 2007). In another study, Hillman, Castelli, & Buck (2005) found that aerobic fitness was positively associated with neuroelectric function and behavioral performance in preadolescent children engaged in a stimulus discrimination task.

Davis et al. (2011) conducted a study on aerobic exercise and executive function in sedentary overweight children and found increased activation in the cerebral cortex after three months of exercise training. Specific gains in mathematics were found in the children who exercised daily for 40 minutes when compared with the children who exercised daily for 20 minutes. The authors note that many questions remain, two are, would the same results hold with lean or healthy children and do the cognitive and academic benefits remain without continued exercise?

According to Dishman et al. (2006), "Motor skill training and regular exercise enhance executive functions of cognition and some types of learning, including motor learning in the spinal cord." "... metabolic and neurochemical pathways among skeletal muscle, the spinal cord, and the brain offer plausible, testable mechanisms that might help explain effects of physical activity and exercise on the central nervous system."

A review of the current literature on the role of acute and chronic exercise on cognitive function suggests more experimentally designed studies are needed.

Motor Development and Cognitive Performance

Current research elucidates our growing understanding of the association between gross motor skill development in the early years with later cognitive performance. This correlation causes one to reflect on the meaning of the relationship between motor development and cognition. Diamond (2000) identified that the critical relationship between motor and cognitive development can be understood when one considers that utilization of the cerebellum and the prefrontal cortex are both necessary for many cognitive functions.

Motor development is an important factor in child development (Bushnell and Boudreau, 1993; Koziol et al., 2014). In the past decade, the relationship between motor and cognitive development has been examined with more frequency. Piek et al. (2008) assessed school-aged children and noted a positive relationship between gross motor skills in the preschool years with later cognitive skills, namely processing speed and working memory in the same cohort in elementary school. Murray et al. (2006) observed a linear relationship between early attainment of the ability to stand in toddlerhood with better cognitive skills in adulthood. Gross motor skill performance at 4 years of age was noted by Son and Meisels (2006) to be positively correlated with better reading and math performance in first grade. Slow motor development in the first year of life was also associated with a smaller vocabulary and slower reading speed in children ages 3–7 (Viholainen et al., 2006).

Cognitive Exercise

Diamond (2015) reviewed the literature on aerobic activity and cognitive performance. Few studies have been conducted on enhancement of executive function through exercise. As it relates to cognition and exercise, we might classify exercise into two categories, simple and cognitive. For our purposes, simple exercise would be aerobic exercise that includes movement with no associated cognitive components, such as running on a treadmill, walking in the park or playing a game of tag.

One can walk or run on a treadmill with automaticity but little necessary thought. In fact, walking at a brisk pace or running on a treadmill might actually have calming effects because one can get into "the zone" and allow their thoughts to wander or even rest.

"Cognitive exercise" as defined in *70 Play Activities* would be a class of movement that is paired with increasingly complex cognitive demands. We prefer motor activities that are well automated such as passing a ball, bouncing a ball, stepping, clapping or marching, depending on the motor skills of the child. The cognitive exercises are always chosen to be relevant to the learning task and might include bouncing a ball while counting or passing a ball while saying words in categories such as types of animals, vocabulary words or state capitals.

Of the studies reviewed by Diamond (2015), one appeared to show executive function benefits through exercise. The specific exercise studied was TaeKwonDo. Lakes and Hoyt (2004) randomly assigned school children to either a traditional PE class or a TaeKwonDo program. Assessment measures after three months of participation showed that the TaeKwonDo participants evidenced statistically significant differences in the areas of cognitive self-regulation, affective self-regulation, prosocial behavior, classroom conduct and performance on a mental math test.

Having played with hundreds of children and done scaffolded "cognitive exercise" with many more, currently I suggest to parents and educators that movement which requires components of specific executive functions (sequencing, simultaneous processing, inhibition, planning, decision-making and problem-solving) such as dance sequences, martial arts sequences, dressage and repetitive targeted tasks, such as specific tennis tasks, may enhance thinking and self-regulation skills in children. But it requires much repeated practice. A single trial is not enough; the child needs to practice enough to develop minimal competency.

It is most useful when the cognitive components are explicitly named, taught and discussed with the students.

As an example we might say to a child with whom we have been working on executive functions for a few sessions, "When we practice a series of three movements in the exercise, such as the one we call 'Tai Chi,' we need to remember the exercises in order, what cognitive process is that? What is it called?" We might go even further: "When we practice a series of three movements in the exercise, such as the one we call 'Tai Chi,' we need to remember the exercises in order, we need to pace them properly and we need to refrain from doing other unnecessary movements. Tai Chi requires us to sequence our actions, pace our actions and inhibit undesirable actions those are three parts of executive functions we use each day for other activities as well such as completing our homework. Let's write down what the exercise Tai Chi and completing our homework have in common so that we can name the executive functions we are using. Now we can examine how we use our executive functions for many specific daily activities. Want to do some more?"

While we have to interpret such a small body of research data with caution, we might hypothesize that an exercise that requires some of the active components of executive function, particularly cognitive activities mediated by the prefrontal cortex, such as planning, organization, sequencing and inhibition, might produce greater "cognitive specific" benefits than exercise that is non-cognitive in nature.

Best concluded, in this review, is that "cognitively-engaging exercise appears to have a stronger effect than non-[cognitively]-engaging exercise on children's executive function[s]." Adele Diamond noted further, "I fully agree. I would like to extend that in several ways. First, I predict that this will be found to be true at all ages, not just in children. Two, I predict that improving bimanual coordination and eye-hand coordination, and working on activities that require frequently crossing the midline and/or rhythmic movement, might be particularly valuable." (Diamond, 2015, p. 2).

What does this mean to clinicians who work with children with neurological, developmental and psychiatric issues in childhood? We need to get moving in therapy and in life. We are best to recognize the importance of movement and activity in brain and behavior change. I reflect on several children I have seen with severe dyslexia who developed into skilled athletes. I believe that "but for" the repeated intense rhythmic quality of the daily training of these athletes in dance and gymnastics, their dyslexia would have been even more impairing.

Entrainment

Entrainment, the natural inclination to join in synchrony with another person or stimulus, is fundamental to biological growth. We entrain sleeping rhythms, motor rhythms and even language patterns. Humans learn and develop a variety of academic, social and cognitive skills via entrainment. We entrain to speech patterns of others, we entrain socially in song and we entrain in motor movement as we walk, play sports, dance, etc. It might be hypothesized that entrainment keeps us safe and connected as social animals. But what happens when we experience difficulty entraining movement or speech? We are observed as being "a little bit off." Our experience with children is that we can help them "be on," with repeated practice of timing, pattern and rhythm tasks that encourage entrainment.

Curiously, I often do some of the ball bouncing exercises in this book with children to either calm or alert them (depending on what they need) before we do executive function, social or academic skills training. When I do an exercise such as "How To Bounce A Ball," most children will synchronize their ball bouncing down beat with me or I will synchronize my ball bouncing with them, over time. It's natural; the body wants synchronicity. If a child with whom I am working does not synchronize after several introductions of this task, I'll then play "down beat" related games such as "Ping and Pong" or "I Clap, You Clap" to see if the child can learn to match movement on a down beat. Generally speaking, synchronizing to a downbeat is easier than synchronizing to an upbeat. If after repeated trials they cannot, I engage our developmental pediatrician or occupational therapy colleagues to do a quality assessment to rule out any related developmental, motor or nervous system delays. For a good review of entrainment, cognition, vibration and temporality see Thaut, McIntosh & Hoemberg (2014): *Neurobiological foundations of neurologic music therapy: rhythmic entrainment and the motor system.*

The Rhythmic Brain

Your brain is rhythmic. It searches for and locks onto rhythmic beats. Rhythm appears to be an organizing feature of the human brain. Even neurons fire in time, to a beat. In research studies, rhythm has been observed to be related to language comprehension, speech production, math and reading.

While the role of rhythm has not been extensively studied in relation to the executive functions, clinically we observe that children with better motor (and auditory) rhythm and timing inhibit their undesirable behavior, plan, sequence and problem-solve better.

The role of rhythm, tempo and timing in language, learning and brain function is garnering more scientific interest. Nina Kraus and Adam Tierney at Northwestern University have studied several aspects of musical brain function and noted in 2014 that musical training improves language and reading skills in children. Reading ability is related to temporal and frequency resolution, rapid auditory processing and phonological awareness. Auditory discrimination of tonality, melody and chord discrimination have been observed to distinguish good readers from poor readers.

Rhythm is also a foundational component to perceiving language and reading. When listening to variations in the rhythmic production of words, children are able to discriminate single words from compound words such as "redshirt" and "red shirt". Being able to track rhythmic patterns is central for speech perception, which in turn is important for the acquisition of reading skills.

Deficits in rhythm or timing may be associated with many aspects of learning and behavior. Poor motor production in association with a rhythm or beat may be a sign of diminished perception and communication between key parts of the brain. Variations in fine and gross motor control, rhythm and timing have been consistently reported in the literature across several diagnostic groups including ADHD, developmental dyslexia, reading and speech language deficits (Schaefer & Overy, 2015; Gordon, Fehd & McCandliss, 2015; Gordon, Magne & Large, 2011; Rosch, Dirlikov & Mostofsky, 2013; Corriveau, Pasquini & Goswami, 2007; Hill, Bishop & Nimmo-Smith, 1998; Zelaznik & Goffman, 2010).

Children with speech language delays, ADHD, and developmental dyslexia have also been observed in studies to have impaired motor production to auditory cues. Auditory discrimination and auditory memory are both critical for learning. A child must hear, discriminate and respond to auditory information throughout the learning process.

Corriveau and Goswami (2009) reported that, "Tapping in synchrony with a beat has been described as the simplest rhythmic act that humans perform." Yet we know that many children with neurodevelopmental diagnoses cannot tap to a beat; they have poor rhythm and they exhibit difficulty matching gross motor output to both rhythm and beat. Like the authors, we observe the presence of subtle impairments in the neural mechanisms for the perception and expression of rhythm and timing which affect normal language, motor and cognitive development. The questions relevant to those of us who play rhythmic musical activities with children are threefold:

1. Can repeated rhythmic patterned motor practice improve neural timing mechanisms as evidenced by improvements in matching motor output to both rhythm and beat?

2. What is the best dose and duration of the rhythmic intervention?

3. Does developing better gross or fine motor rhythm and timing improve subsequent learning (academic or behavioral)?

We are excited about future research related to the role of rhythm, patterns and timing in learning and behavior. While the research is ongoing, we have children in our offices and classrooms who are ready to play. What follows are activities we have developed to enhance what I call The Fab 4: thinking, self-regulation, learning and behavior.

Executive Functions (EF)

Ah, executive functions: two words we read about a lot these days. What are they and why do they matter? The executive functions include a number of interrelated higher order cognitive processes necessary for the purposeful and goal-directed behavior that allows us to be successful social animals. There are a wide variety of definitions for executive functions, written about in a broad manner by many researchers (Das, Meltzer, Goldberg, Dawson, Barkley, Rief, Guare, Brown, Naglieri, McCloskey, Miller, Keeley, etc.).

When we define executive functions in *70 Play Activities*, we are usually doing so with three purposes in mind:

1. To communicate with parents and teachers about the strengths and weaknesses in a specific child's skill competencies.

2. To clarify for the members of a treatment, education or intervention team what skills we are working on and how we define them.

3. To develop treatment, education and intervention plans that will help the child to enhance much needed skill sets.

When we implement 70 Play Activities, we generally think of executive functions as follows:

METACOGNITION

- **THINKING ABOUT THINKING** - The act of recognizing that one possesses thoughts, then reflecting on what those thoughts are.

- **CRITICAL THINKING** - Analyzing, decoding and examining thoughts, knowledge, actions, feelings and experiences.

- **CREATIVE THINKING** - Generating new or novel ideas. Reshaping, reframing and taking action on knowledge, information and activities in a new or novel manner.

- **APPLYING PAST KNOWLEDGE** - Using what one has learned or knows to learn novel content, problem-solve, make decisions, think, speak or act.

ORGANIZATION

- **MANAGEMENT OF MATERIALS** - The physical organization, labeling, categorizing and placement of specific materials or tools (clothing, school supplies, sporting equipment etc.)

- **MANAGEMENT OF DAILY TASKS** - The strategy and approach to successful management of the daily activities of life (hygiene, eating, sleeping, household chores, school work, sports, etc.)

- **MANAGEMENT OF LONG-TERM PROJECTS** - The ability to preview, plan, allocate time and execute the components that make up a larger constellation of tasks, to one end goal.

TASK MANAGEMENT

- **PLANNING** - The act of strategizing to take action in a meaningful, purposeful and goal-directed manner.

- **PREVIEWING** - Using simultaneous processing to consider the entirety of all the components of a task or activity, in order to think about, plan and prepare to take action.

- **PRIORITIZING** - Considering the imminence and importance of a task or a series of tasks in order to determine what to take action upon first.

- **INITIATION** - Beginning a defined task, activity or action.

- **EXECUTION** - Taking goal-directed action in order to effect or complete a specific task, activity or action.

- **REVIEWING** - Reflecting on the components of a task, activity, action or response in order to examine the utility, efficacy and outcome of an task, event or experience.

- **REVISING** - Using the knowledge gained from reviewing in order to revise one's future actions.

- **COMPLETING** - Bringing a task, activity or action to a successful ending.

TIME MANAGEMENT

- **TIME ESTIMATION** - Predicting, imagining or estimating the time it will take to successfully complete a specific task, activity or action.

- **TIME MONITORING** - Experiencing an accurate assessment of the passage of time while executing a specific task, activity or action.

- **TIME ALLOCATION** - Distributing a finite amount of time to a specific task, activity or action.

- **PROJECT PLANNING** - Planning for the successful completion of components of several tasks that will contribute to the completion of a larger task, experience or event.

ATTENTION

- **ALERTING** - Moving to a state of cognitive readiness.

- **SELECTING** - Moving one's attention and focus to a specific target stimulus.

- **ATTENDING** - Directing meaningful energy and attention to a specific target stimulus.

- **SUSTAINING** - Maintaining attention on a specific target stimulus, long enough to take action on it.

- **MONITORING DRIFT** - Observing the mind becoming off-task.

- **RE-ALERTING** - Bringing attention back online.

- **DIVIDING** - Maintaining attention to two related tasks within a brief period of time.

- **ALTERNATING** - Shifting attention from one target stimulus to another within a brief period of time.

- **DISENGAGING** - Withdrawing one's attention or focus from a specific stimulus.

- **RE-DIRECTING** - Shifting attention from one stimulus to another with purpose or intent.

COGNITIVE CONTROL

- **PERSISTENCE** - Adhering to a task or course of action without hesitation, in spite of obstacles.

- **SHIFT** - Putting aside one thought, feeling or action and replacing it with another.

- **FLEXIBILITY** - Shifting emotional valence to a thought, feeling or action with positivity; refraining from becoming rigid or stuck.

- **DISTRACTIBILITY** - Diverting attention away from a salient stimulus to another, often non-relevant stimulus; losing focus.

MEMORY

- **WORKING MEMORY** - The cognitive system responsible for transiently holding or maintaining necessary information or data ready-at-hand for relatively immediate access, in a short period of time.

- **PROCESSING** - The cognitive act of perceiving and responding to a stimulus, often under time constraints.

- **SHORT-TERM MEMORY** - The cognitive system responsible for the holding of information for a limited amount of time, usually less than several minutes.

- **LONG-TERM MEMORY** - The cognitive system responsible for the storage of information for the long term, often permanently.

- **STORING** - The process of consolidating cognitive, motor or emotional knowledge.

- **ENCODING** - Taking information into the memory system and registering it as meaningful in preparation for storage or retrieval.

- **RETRIEVAL** - Accessing previously stored information.

- **UTILIZATION** - Taking action on previously stored information.

- **SYNTHESIZING** - Combining parts of information or knowledge for action, utilization or meaningful application.

PROBLEM-SOLVING - The process of working through details of a problem to reach a solution.

DECISION-MAKING - The thought process of selecting a logical choice from the available options.

EMOTIONAL REGULATION - The ability to respond, in a measured manner, to life circumstances and experiences.

- **RECOGNITION** - To be aware of a change in internal energy states or emotions.

- **IDENTIFICATION** - To know, recognize or understand a specific emotion or feeling.

- **LABELING** - To put a meaningful name or category to an energy or emotional state.

- **CATEGORIZING** - To make sense of an emotional experience by placing it in a group or category with past experiences, circumstances or situations.

- **ESCALATION** - An increase in an internal energy state related to the emotional response to an experience, circumstance or situation.

- **DE-ESCALATION** - A decrease in an internal energy state related to the emotional response to an experience, circumstance or situation.

IMPULSE CONTROL - The ability to manage one's urges.

- **INHIBITION** - The process of showing restraint; stopping a word, thought or action.

- **DISINHIBITION** - Showing a lack of cognitive, emotional or motor restraint.

MOTOR MANAGEMENT - The ability to control the motor elements of movement, pace, speed, direction, timing, etc.

- **PLANNING** - The ability to plan and carry out a specific motor action.

- **PACING** - The speed at which one exhibits a motor action.

- **RHYTHM** - A repeated pattern of sounds and silence in speech, sound or movement.

- **TIMING** - The ability to activate one's motor movements to coincide with an internal or external beat.

- **INITIATING** - Beginning or starting a motor movement.

- **MAINTAINING** - Continuing to exhibit a motor movement over time.

- **STOPPING** - To cease a motor movement.

When providing the children with information about how their brains work, here are some of the skills we discuss with them. We print out the list and let the children circle the ones they feel we are working on. We explore what each executive function is and how it helps us learn and behave better. We ask the children to explain how their brain is using the specific skill. Then they can teach us (and others) how their brain works with more confidence and specificity as they participate in the activities.

- Alerting Attention
- Applying Past Knowledge
- Balance
- Cognitive Flexibility
- Cognitive Persistence
- Coordination
- Creative Thinking
- Critical Thinking
- Decision-Making
- Emotional Regulation
- Exploration
- Focused Attention
- Impulse Control
- Inhibition
- Memory Strategy
- Motor Management
- Motor Planning
- Motor Sequencing
- Narrative Language

- Organization
- Planning
- Previewing
- Prioritizing
- Problem-Solving
- Project Planning
- Reflection
- Rhythm
- Sequencing
- Successive Processing
- Sustained Attention
- Task Management
- Time Allocation
- Time Estimation
- Time Monitoring
- Visual Scanning
- Visual Working Memory
- Working Memory

You Are Here to PLAY
So Let's Dive In!

Teaching Children About How Their Brains Work

chapter 2

In this brief chapter, we discuss how important it is to include the children as co-creators, mentors and educators when you play *70 Play Activities*. In fact, there is a body of literature in the field of cognitive education which confirms that when you teach children about how their brains work, they learn better.

In Chapter 3, we will get to the crux of much of the foundation of this book, a concept we call Musical Thinking. Musical Thinking is the primary method we use to teach children the cognitive science behind how they learn.

Why We Teach Kids How Their Brains Work

Involving children in the generation, implementation and revision of cognitive and executive function interventions seems rather new. In current literature, neuroscientists and educators are just beginning to reference its value. Actually, the research supporting the notion that we need to teach children not only "content" but the "process" by which their brains work, dates back to Plato (Haywood, 2013). It was then advanced by Alexander Luria, Lev Vygotsky and subsequent researchers including J. P. Das, co-author of *Cognitive Planning and Executive Functions: Applications in Education & Management* and Carl Haywood, co-author of *Bright Start: Cognitive Curriculum for Young Children*.

In his 2013 article, *What Is Cognitive Education? The View from 30,000 Feet*, Dr. H. Carl Haywood reviews the history and efficacy of cognitive education research, pointing out that the emphasis on creating systems for thinking is thousands of years old. The act of engaging the mind in critical thinking, reflection and problem-solving enhances both learning and cognition. While we have known this for a long time, we clearly need to include children more in the process of developing, revising, teaching and mentoring neurocognitive interventions.

Several of the cognitive education curriculums that have been studied since the 1980s are Bright Start, PREP, Cogent, Cognitive Enrichment Advantage and Tools of The Mind. Back in the 1990s there were programs such as Bright Start in which "one brief class period per day is devoted to lessons that are sharply focused on processes of thinking and learning, whereas the rest of the school day is devoted to lessons and activities with a focus on academic content," (Haywood, 2013, p. 29). We hope *70 Play Activities* encourages educators around the world to incorporate strategies and activities that show children how their brains work. When we show children the "Why and How" of learning, they are more invested in the process. It is quite empowering for them. When we go beyond teaching the "content" in education and teach children the tools and strategies for better executive function, while explaining the cognitive reasons for what we do and how we do it, we dramatically improve their learning.

- We raise students who are better thinkers, planners, decision-makers and problem-solvers.
- We reduce the stigma of learning differences by showing children that we all process information differently.
- With greater ease, we better tailor education to each individual student.
- We better prepare children for the Enterprise era yet to come – a time when people will occupy roles and jobs currently not known to us (primarily resulting from major advances in technology).
- We enhance brain development by making children more active learners, mentors and teachers.
- We raise children who enjoy their own educational experience.
- We make learning meaningful.

Neurologist Frederic Perez-Alvarez and educational psychologist Carme Timoneda-Gallart, authors of *A Better Look at Intelligent Behavior (2007)*, observed in their dyslexia treatment clinic that when they taught their child patients "How Your Brain Works" using videos they produced called FUNDI, the children appeared better able to find the reading and executive function interventions more meaningful. The children also invested more concerted energy in the brain building tasks and felt more empowered to take charge of their learning skills.

When we Teach

children about how their brain works and why a particular activity or task will improve their thinking, learning or behavior, they become an integral part of the learning process. Their knowledge and active involvement in understanding why they are being asked to do a specific academic task makes them more motivated learners.

A common complaint heard from students is, "Why do I need to learn this? How will it help me?" **If children were taught, "It is the process of how you think, not simply the content that you learn, that will help define success and happiness in your life," children would be more motivated to learn**. The emphasis on content learning and testing is weighing our children down. Let us honor and engage the children we teach by introducing them to neuroscientific concepts to help them understand how their brain works and how learning happens. When children know the "why" and "how" behind what they are doing, they participate more enthusiastically and learn better.

How We Teach Kids How Their Brains Work

As educators, we teach children about how their brains work by introducing the fact that our brain thinks, organizes, remembers and learns using a system of skills called executive functions.

There are four important parts to what we do.

1. We discuss executive functions as a group of skills our brains employ to help us become successful people.

2. We teach children to know, recognize and label some of the executive functions or cognitive processes they are using during a given task.

3. We empower children to take better command of their thinking, self-regulation, learning and behavior by teaching them the cognitive science behind how their brains learn.

4. We enhance the automaticity of their executive functions with play, gamification and movement leading to greater levels of motivation and participation as well as more deeply ingrained skill sets.

Instead of writing the executive functions up on the board and going through the definitions, we have created over 70 "games" or activities that help the children not only use specific executive functions, but understand the importance of these executive functions. While we do the activities, we often discuss what executive functions are and how we use them. We call this the "direct instruction" part of our work, as we readily define executive functions with the children, making their cognitive processes more transparent to them. When we take the mystery out of how the children think, teaching them about neuroscience, they respond with enthusiasm and confidence. You can do the same simply by helping the children to be "knowing" about how their cognitive processes work.

The motor-based activities have benefits as well. With movement, we make the cognitive, social-emotional and self-regulatory skills more automated and more deeply embedded in the cerebellum. Research supports that when we open neural pathways with repetition, critical cognitive skills, which we refer to as executive functions, become more automated, leading to more efficient and successful learning.

These games and activities may strengthen executive functioning simply by practicing the sub-tasks of executive function over and over again. However, what they really help with is building a child's awareness of his or her cognitive abilities. The activities provide an opportunity to apply executive skills through games, play and practice. They help the child become mindful of thinking things through, taking time to encode knowledge into memory, plan, sequence and organize content and actions. The activities demystify what executive functions look like, feel like and work like in real life. The transparency of these learning objectives is a key component in supporting children to have greater metacognitive awareness.

Musical Thinking

chapter 3

The foundation of *70 Play Activities* is a cognitive empowerment strategy I call "Musical Thinking." Although not every activity in this book is a derivative of musical thinking, most could be. And when you see why, I hope you say, "Wow! this is cool." I have to say, from the outset, that I am not a musician. I can play about four chords each on the guitar and piano. But I am musical, and soon you will find out you are too.

Research provides us with a new understanding about the key role of rhythm and patterns in the development of early learning. The importance of foundational aspects of music, tempo, rhythm and timing is now becoming clear. Musical tempo, rhythm and timing are among the first patterning experiences children have, beginning when we play simple hand games like "Peek-a-boo" and "Pat-a-cake" when children are toddlers. We then move on to hiding games like "Where is thumbkin"? Next, songs and simple nursery rhymes like "I'm a little teapot," and "Itsy bitsy spider" introduce patterns in language and movement combined with cognition and working memory games. These activities are central to early learning but, by about six years of age, they fall out of favor in curricula. They are considered "nursery games" when really they are important life-long learning games. Music provides a highly social, natural and developmentally appropriate way for children to engage the critical executive functions they will use throughout elementary and middle school. Therefore, we need to incorporate musical patterns, tempo, rhythm and timing in the daily academic lives of children.

Musical Thinking is a cognitive empowerment strategy that evolved out of my playing math and reading with children as a parent volunteer at our local elementary school. I observed that most of the children with math and reading difficulties exhibited poor timing output. When they read aloud, their oral fluency was stilted and when they computed math equations they appeared rushed and scattered. Even as a parent, it was easy to see that they needed strategies to improve their approach to and execution of daily academic tasks.

So I started to play simple made-up games with them to slow them down and help them think through problems. I'd say things like, "Let's read this sentence as though we are turtles," or "Let's walk like giant giraffes while we add some numbers together." Over time, Musical Thinking evolved to be what it is today. I know it will change and improve even more as we all play with more children, but for now the system is very useful and the children love it. That's what matters most.

We can keep teaching the tempo, rhythm and timing that underlie reading, writing, mathematics and behavior with children after six years of age by playing games with cognitive and motor components. Several schools do this with math raps, musical storytelling, dance and movement.

We do it more systematically with Musical Thinking. With Musical Thinking, we teach children about critical executive functions while helping them experience what the tempo, rhythm and timing feel like. We see Musical Thinking as scaffolding, like a large pine tree on which the children can meaningfully hang the executive functions and use them as they need them.

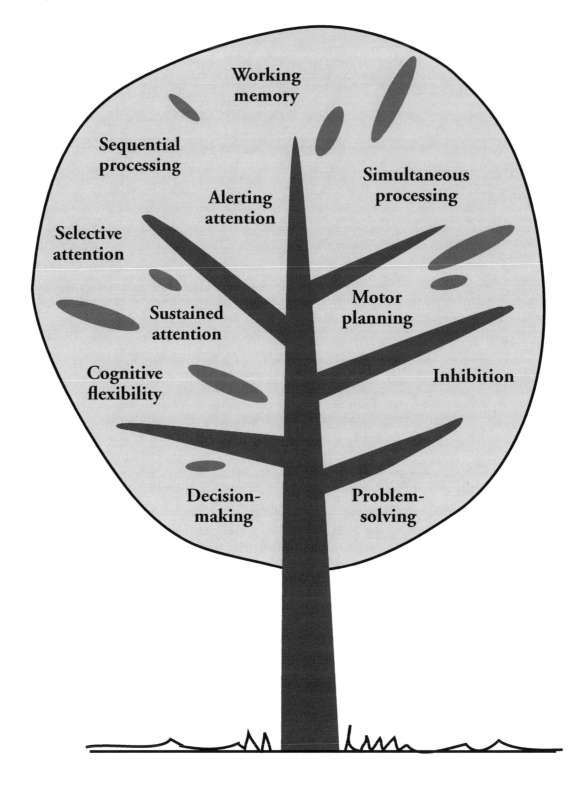

Motor Exploration, Musical Compositions and Cognitive Applications

With Musical Thinking, we help the children practice important executive function skills, name executive function skills and become empowered to choose to use and develop their executive function skills. Musical Thinking activities are divided into three sections: Motor Exploration, Musical Compositions and Cognitive Applications. With the time limitations we often experience in therapy and the classroom, you may feel rushed to move right to the cuing and thinking questions in the Cognitive Applications section, but I urge you to begin with Motor Exploration, as the movement, rhythm and music are what prime the brain for cognitive skill learning. Entrainment, syncopation and vibration accelerate learning for some children. Further, the Motor Exploration and Musical Composition activities create motivation and "buy-in" from the children because they are learning in such a creative, playful and engaging manner. We encourage you to pick and choose, move around the activities and use your own teaching and clinical experience to apply the more than 30 activities.

So, instead of telling you about it, let's do it. **Let's play Musical Thinking**.

Introduction to Musical Thinking Motor Exploration

Okay, stand up. Now, right where you are, in your office, classroom or in front of your computer, start marching. Think of a marching band and simply march in place. Step 1-2-3-4, 1-2-3-4. Try counting your steps out loud. 1-2-3-4, 1-2-3-4. Excellent. If you are a musician you know that you are actually marching to a time signature; in this case, the time signature is 4/4 time. For every "measure" of music you are taking four steps:, those steps are four beats. Now try this: step on your right foot for two beats and then your left foot for two beats. It sounds like **1**-2; **3**-4. Let's step on each foot for two counts for eight total counts. So it will feel like **1**-2; **3**-4; **5**-6; **7**-8. Perfect!

> We have found that some exercises, particularly when they include movement, are easier to understand when you can see them. Therefore, we have made videos of many of the exercises. They can be found on Dr. Kenney's
> YouTube Channel http://bit.ly/Bloom4

VIDEO 1: What is it – MT Intro, what is it, how is it musical, why do we do it? We may not have time to become skilled musicians, but we do have the time to execute simple exercises that rely on the components of music most associated with cognitive function, rhythm, tempo, timing and beat.

VIDEO 2: **What are the Love Notes and how do we use them?**

VIDEO 3: Modes of communication. Teaching executive functions with music, notation, composition and visuals. Hear it, feel it, write it, create it.

VIDEO 4: How does MT teach EF?

 VIDEO 5: Where to begin – Establishing the quarter note beat, why we start here and how to do it.

So you stepped or marched two measures of four beats each as well as two measures of two beats each. Let's put it all together. You step 1-2-3-4; 1-2-3-4; 1-2; 3-4; 1-2; 3-4. Did you count the measures? Try it again; this time count the measures. March 1-2-3-4; 1-2-3-4; 1-2; 3-4; 1-2; 3-4. Did you march five measures? Did you march eight measures? How many measures did you march? That's right, you marched four measures.

VIDEO 6: Establishing the half-note beat.

See – you are musical. **When you marched four beats to a measure, you were actually marching in quarter notes.** You can feel it, right? Pretty cool, eh? **Then, when you marched two beats per measure, you marched in half notes.** Children adore this. They love to learn that they are musical. They love to relate to numbers in a way that is fun, engaging, meaningful and not stressful. When you play with children and show them that their natural rhythms tend to move in quarter notes and half notes, they begin to change. They read differently, understand math differently, learn better and behave better. I'll show you some examples of this in a bit.

For now, in Musical Thinking, we have two more notes to explore. The first is the whole note. The whole note has one beat that lasts the duration of the measure. So the whole notes goes 1 x x x ; 1 x x x. You can try it; simply stand on one foot for four counts, then the other foot for four counts. That's what a whole note feels like.

VIDEO 7: Establishing the whole note beat.

Then there is the rest sign, which we actually make the fourth note in Musical Thinking. The children with whom we play guided this decision and it has worked really well. We are using our imaginations; we know a rest sign is not a note in real music, but it has meaning like a note and it embodies the "we all need time to rest" message so important in learning.

Increasingly, research tells us that after we think, we need a time of rest to integrate and store the information we learned. The moment of rest allows us to make meaning of the information and store it in memory. Rest has been shown to take place wakefully within hours of learning, as well as during sleep via Resting State Networks (Albert, Robertson & Miall, 2009).

In real music, each type of note, a quarter note, half note, whole note, etc., has its own symbol for rest. In Musical Thinking, we use the quarter note rest signal for all of our work. Why? First, we want to make Musical Thinking easy enough that a six-year-old can understand it. Second, the quarter note is the central note in all our work. Children often move around their worlds in quarter notes; quarter notes are notes kids easily understand. All you need to do is watch a second-grade class walk from their classroom to the lunch room and you will observe them walking in quarter notes.

 VIDEO 8: The rest note.

Alright, if your brain is spinning, simply stand up and walk in quarter notes and half notes. Make up a few patterns, relax, enjoy, move softly, you'll calm right down.

When Would You Use Musical Thinking?

Musical Thinking is applicable to a variety of activities related to thinking, self-regulation, behavior and learning.

IN THERAPY:

On occasion, clinicians ask us, "When would I do Musical Thinking or the Movement Activities?" Curiously, while therapists are often taught to dive into the training as soon as "rapport" has been established, we have learned, over time, that many children need a transitional time before the cognitive work of social, academic and behavioral skill instruction to become alert or calmed in order to learn the new skills. Therefore, we enter into the session for 8–10 minutes and close the session for 5–8 minutes with either altering or calming activities, be they drumming, marching, clapping or even compositions. The entrance into the therapeutic hour with rhythm, movements and sounds, which are child-derived, deepens the learning opportunity.

IN THE CLASSROOM:

In the classroom, we use the Musical Thinking activities first thing in the morning, after lunch and often at the end of the day to prepare the children for transitions into after-school activities. We also use the Musical Thinking activities as "cognitive exercise" when we layer content over motor movements. This kind of learning is called motor-cognition. Examples include marching while students say their vocabulary words, learning spelling words in half-notes and recalling spelling words in quarter notes as well as practicing history facts with Musical Thinking Compositions.

We choose the activity based on the needs of the students or class as a whole. It's important to know that many of the movement and rhythm activities in this book can be used to either alert or calm. If you do activities quickly they tend to be alerting; slow them down and they tend to be calming. But each child is different; we have seen some children who are alerted by yoga moves and others who are almost put to sleep. The body and brain do what each child needs, and sometimes that is simply rest.

Once children understand the foundational concepts **Rhythm, Tempo** (pace) and **Timing**, you can teach children most of the executive functions – academic content, study skills, self-management, social interaction, mood modulation, motor movement and more – using Musical Thinking. Here is a little story, just to get our feet wet.

PERIWINKLE AND PACE

SPOTLIGHT STORY

Brennan is a nine-year-old who is very excited to come to school each day. His teacher has a pet lizard in the classroom named Periwinkle, whom Brennan adores. Brennan literally flies out of bed each morning because he knows that he will soon be in school with Periwinkle by his side. The challenge is that in his enthusiasm, he can be a spot rough with the lizard. He reaches quickly into the cage and grabs at the lizard, scaring it. His teacher has used verbal explanations, peer modeling and rewards to help Brennan approach Periwinkle with a softer touch. But words like "slow down," "touch gently," and "be careful" have not resulted in the desired change.

One day the teacher asked Brennan, "Brennan how fast do you walk?" He just looked at her bewildered. Then she said, "Do you walk Quick or Slow?" Brennan responded, "I walk Super Quick." Brennan's teacher then asked Brennan to show her what super quick looked like and Brennan sped around the room like a roadrunner. She then clapped her hands accompanying his walking speed and told him, "It's true Brennan, you are walking Super Super Quick. What will it look like if you walk more slowly?" She joined Brennan in practicing different motor paces, Super Quick, Quick, Slow and Super Slow. They walked around the room, playfully moving at different paces. All the while, she was labeling their movements and asking him questions, "If I walk this fast am I walking Super Super Quick or Quick?"

After a bit, she began tapping on the desk with her hands, also reflecting on the speed and intensity of her movement, and she asked Brennan to tap along. "Are we tapping the desk Quick or Super Quick?" As Brennan followed along, she slowed down her pace and reflected, "Brennan how are we tapping now? Are we tapping Slow or Super Slow?" Brennan said, "Super Slow." "Brennan, let's really feel how slow Super Slow is." "Can we do a few other things in the room right now Super Slowly?" Then they pretended to walk on the moon at a Super Slow pace. They reached for a pencil at a Super Slow pace. She let Brennan lead as much as possible and used her narrative language to cue, describe and even alter his pace.

Now it was time to talk about Periwinkle. "Brennan, it's been fun to have you show me how fast we do things in our classroom. I learned from you that we can choose how fast we do things. Let's talk for a moment about Periwinkle. Does she move Super Quick or Super Slow?" Brennan said, "She barely moves at all." The teacher smiled and said, "That's right, she mostly just sits there. When she does move, like to eat a cricket, how does she move?" "Oh, Super Slow," answered Brennan. "So it sounds like she feels best moving Super Slow. Does that tell us anything about how she wants us to move with her?" "Yes, she probably likes it when we move Super Slow," Brennan said.

The teacher and Brennan then practiced approaching Periwinkle's cage at a Slow Pace, opening the cage at a Super Slow pace and reaching in to pet the lizard at a Slow pace.

Brennan and his class were introduced to Musical Thinking soon after. They learned the visual and motor cues, they learned how to label their movement, thinking and learning and Brennan was able to think of actions both in terms of pace "Quick or Slow" and in terms of Rhythm, which we will discuss later.

How We Teach Musical Thinking To Children

Current research demonstrates that musical training in children is associated with heightening of sound sensitivity related to enhancement in verbal abilities and general reasoning skills. Children who participate in musical instrument education have better auditory discrimination and earn better grades than non-musicians. Musical training is also related to phonological processing, as well as math achievement (Wetter, Koerner & Schwaninger, 2009; Gordon, Fehd & McCandliss, 2015; Kraus et al., 2014b; Leong & Goswami, 2014; Miendlarzewska & Trost, 2013). According to Miendlarzewska & Trost, learning to play an instrument as a child may even predict academic performance and IQ in young adulthood. Music training correlates with plastic changes in auditory, motor, and sensorimotor integration areas of the brain. As the research grows, we seek to know more about the role of socio-economic, leadership, teaching, community, social, family and genetic factors related to music and learning.

Fundamentally, we believe, based on our interactions with children, that musical training, physical movement, creative play and direct executive function skill instruction are beneficial for children. Further, we observe that some of the foundational cognitive skills taught in music instruction (choral and instrumental), such as sequencing (motor, visual and auditory), simultaneous processing, memory, temporal organization, auditory discrimination and inhibition, are beneficial to child development, learning and behavior. We would like to see musical training, such as Shelle Soelberg's "Let's Play Music," France's "Meludia" as well as musical instrument programs, movement and dance, available for all children beginning in preschool. Our current solution, given that we have children in our schools and practices who need help now, before more research is conducted and educational policy changes are made, is Musical Thinking. We posit that we can introduce some of the elements of musical training to children, such as tempo, rhythm, timing and movement, to enhance executive function skills through creative play to improve learning and behavior.

In Musical Thinking we show the children that their natural rhythm is associated with learning. Specifically, the pace at which we walk, clap or march is directly associated with four concepts critical to memory and learning: encoding, retrieval, processing and consolidation. We then apply this concept of Musical Thinking to all sorts of thinking, learning and self-regulation skills.

Because we want each child to experience how "thinking feels," that is, what it feels like to slow down to process information or speed up to recall information, we help the child experience rhythm, tempo and timing with motor movement. We begin by asking the children in the class (or one-on-one in therapy or at home) to stand up and begin marching in place. Because we know that tempo, rhythm and timing are integrally tied to cognitive processing, we playfully march encouraging the children to seek the same rhythm.

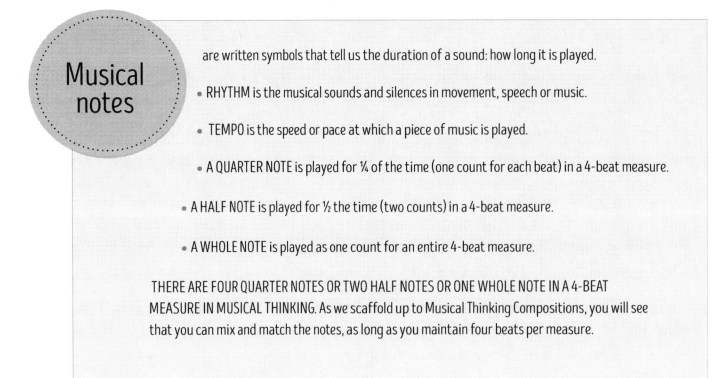

Musical notes

are written symbols that tell us the duration of a sound: how long it is played.

- RHYTHM is the musical sounds and silences in movement, speech or music.

- TEMPO is the speed or pace at which a piece of music is played.

- A QUARTER NOTE is played for ¼ of the time (one count for each beat) in a 4-beat measure.

- A HALF NOTE is played for ½ the time (two counts) in a 4-beat measure.

- A WHOLE NOTE is played as one count for an entire 4-beat measure.

THERE ARE FOUR QUARTER NOTES OR TWO HALF NOTES OR ONE WHOLE NOTE IN A 4-BEAT MEASURE IN MUSICAL THINKING. As we scaffold up to Musical Thinking Compositions, you will see that you can mix and match the notes, as long as you maintain four beats per measure.

As you read through the Musical Thinking activities, you will see numbers that count out beats. Each number, sound or movement is made on the downbeat. When one is marching, the downbeat is when the foot hits the ground. When we are passing balls, hand to hand, the downbeat is when the ball is transferred to the other hand. When we are bouncing balls, the beat is when the ball hits the target, be it the ground, the hands of the other person, table or floor. We use the symbol + to show the "and" in the musical sequence. So if two people are bouncing a ball, the "and" is when the other person catches the ball. We use an x to denote a beat that is being counted but not tapped, clapped or marched. So if we are counting half notes it looks like 1 x 2 x. Occasionally we use the word (hold) if the notation is getting too complicated, that reads like 1 (hold), 2 (hold). We usually do not make sounds on the x but we might nod our heads or bend our knees for added cuing when the child needs additional rhythmic support. You shall experience the beat as we move along, so worry not, the rhythm is in your DNA; your body will understand even before your mind does.

Let's Start with Activity #1!
LET'S MARCH!

Musical Thinking - Motor Exploration
LET'S MARCH!

Activating the brain's natural inclination to seek entrainment, in this case motor synchronization, we begin to step at the same pace as an entire class or with a child in the clinical hour. The rate at which we step becomes about 85 beats per minute. We may use cuing and count it out. You can also use a metronome or drums to model for the children what 85 beats per minute sounds like.

QUARTER NOTES

"Let's march 1-2-3-4; 1-2-3-4."

After marching a minute or so, the teacher asks a student, "Are you a musician?" The student may reply yes or no. If the student replies "no" the teacher says, "That's interesting because you look like a musician." If the student replies "yes," the teacher responds, "I can see that." In both instances the teacher's next reply is, "Isn't it cool that you are marching in quarter notes. So now we can feel what it's like to march to a quarter note."

QUICK NOTES

"Now, we could feel that quarter note as 'Quick.' We could say Quick, Quick, Quick, Quick. Because we are going to learn four notes today and the first one is called the quarter note, it is also a Quick note and we generally march four quarter notes or quick notes in a row."

▶ **VIDEO 9: Quick and Slow.**

HALF NOTES

The class marches a bit more and then the teacher asks, "So, if right now we are marching in quarter notes, what would it look like if we walked in half notes?" The students then march in half-time at approximately 50 beats per minute. As the students step on one foot for two counts then the other foot for two counts the teacher counts "1-2, 3-4." Take your time here. For some children, getting the rhythm may be difficult. Using counting as a cue usually helps. You can count out many steps, even 32 or 64; step with the students until you are all on the same beat. Have fun, move slowly – we want the children to enjoy this process and see it as natural, not difficult.

SLOW NOTES

When it is time to naturally pause, let the children stand still and tell them that, "We could say we are walking, marching or stepping in half notes. We can also call them 'Slow.' Because they are half as fast as quarter notes, which we call 'Quick', half notes are 'Slow.'" We know the half notes are not exactly half of 85 beats per minute, but having played with hundreds of children, about 50 beats per minute feels slow to them, so that's how we define a half note as about 50 beats per minute.

Now as a group or within the clinical hour, you can revel with them about how musical they are. Kids who never before saw themselves as musical might now.

"Wow! So we can march or walk in quarter notes or half notes."

Note: We understand 50 is not half of 85, so I hope that doesn't frustrate you. But having played with hundreds of children, 50 beats per minute feels quite slow to them. You may shift the beats per minute as you wish, 85 BPM and 50 BPM are not written in stone; they are what we have come to, by mutual agreement with the children, over time. If you have a child who prefers 85 BPM and 42.5 BPM that's fine with us. In fact, years ago when we played Musical Thinking Quick was 100 beats per minute, but we came across too many children for whom that was simply too fast. So be flexible, collaborate with the children with whom you work, particularly after they understand Musical Thinking well, and shift beats per minute to suit your student's or client's needs.

Activity #2

Musical Thinking – Motor Exploration
COUNTING MUSICAL SETS

We can also count musical "sets" – groups of measures of beats. As the children are marching or stepping out quarter notes, the teacher can encourage them to count with her, "**1**-2-3-4; **2**-2-3-4; **3**-2-3-4; **4**-2-3-4." Any movements can be counted in sets; it's a great way to get the class or client energized with movement and simultaneous counting. You can even yell, clap, stomp, jump or hop on the first count or do a move on one of the counts, with emphasis, to help the children experience beats, tempo and timing. See the list of movement ideas at the end of this chapter. They will inspire you to make up your own sets or sequences.

 VIDEO 10: Counting Sets.

Measures of music have an interesting correlation to cognitive processing. We learn by understanding the sequences of content, knowledge or actions. When we think about the steps it takes to, for example, pack a backpack for school, we exhibit a series of actions: put the backpack on a hard surface, unzip the backpack, make sure it is empty, place the first book in, place the next book in, place your folder in, place your pencils in, etc. The same is true of reading a book, practicing our math facts or even brushing our teeth before we sleep. Helping children to experience the "sets" of sequences of activities in their daily lives improves their approach to tasks as well as their task execution. Sequencing enhances organization; clapping, stepping, marching or even singing musical sequences is fun as well as great for learning.

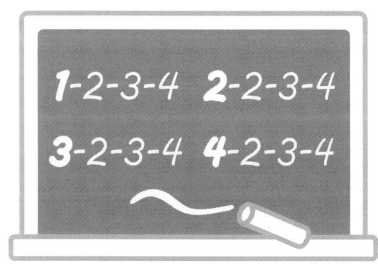

Activity #3

Musical Thinking - Motor Exploration
QUARTER NOTE RETRIEVAL

"You know how we learned how to walk or march in quarter notes and half notes? Well, this is interesting because you know how we have been talking about our executive functions and how they are brain processes we use to learn? Now we are experiencing two cognitive processes, they are called encoding and retrieval. BIG words, we know. Encoding and retrieval actually refer to how you put information into your brain, you encode. Then, how you take it out of your brain, you retrieve. We actually encode information in half notes and retrieve well-learned information in quarter notes."

"Let's see this in action. We can stand up and march just like we did before. Let's march 1-2-3-4; 1-2-3-4. Now if I ask you to say the names of all the capitals of the states in the United States alphabetically each time you step on a beat, would that be easy or hard? That's right, it would be super difficult because you would have to think of all the capitals, alphabetize them and then say them. You could not simply retrieve them, you would actually have to perform 'cognitive operations' thinking, remembering, organizing then retrieving."

"But, if I ask you to count to 100, beginning with 1, each time you step on a beat, 1-2-3-4-5-6-7-8-9-10, etc, you could do that pretty easily. Why? Because the numbers 1–100 are stored in your memory. You know how to count to 100, so you can do it rather quickly in quarter notes. You retrieve what is well-learned quickly because it is consolidated in your memory."

"Let's try to retrieve some information from our brains in quarter notes and see how we do. First, let's walk in quarter notes and simply count to 50. We will say one number for each beat. Ready, count, '1-2-3-4-5-6-7-8-9-10-11-12-13-14-15-16-17-18-19-20. . ..' Great!"

"In fact, you might even be able to retrieve highly automated information even faster, in eighth notes. Pretty cool, right? Let's count by ones to twenty really fast and you will feel the difference between quarter notes and eighth notes." "Terrific! So it's a pretty awesome way for us to know how well we are learning something. If we can retrieve it in eighth notes, we know it crazy well! If we retrieve it in quarter notes, we know it very well, certainly well enough to take a test on it. If we are still learning, we retrieve it more slowly in half-notes and that is just fine! Learning has to start somewhere and slow learning is deeper learning."

"Do you think we could skip count by 2's in quarter notes? For some of us our 2's are deeply embedded in our long-term memory, so we could retrieve them in quarter notes, let's give it a try. For every beat, we will say a number beginning with 2. Ready? Go! 2-4-6-8-10-12-14-16-18-20. . .." "Let's learn another cool way our brain works. We encode, take information in and store it, in half notes. Sometimes we even need to use whole notes if the information is complex;, we'll do that in a bit."

Activity #4

Musical Thinking – Motor Exploration
HALF NOTE ENCODING

"So, we have learned a bit about quarter notes and half notes. One thing we know is that a half note is slower than a quarter note, it is half as fast. So while a quarter note can be known as 'Quick, Quick, Quick, Quick.' a half note is 'Slow, Slow.' The half note is two beats per note, or two quarter notes. Let's feel the half note again so we can see how we learn information or encode information in half notes. We can step on one foot for two counts then the other foot for two counts, **1**-2, **3**-4. Let's try that for two measures. Two measures will be eight beats, step on one foot for two counts then the other foot for two counts. **1**-2, **3**-4; **1**-2, **3**-4."

"If we were learning something new, let's say skip counting 3's, we would learn these numbers in half notes. We would say as we step or march, 3 (hold) 6 (hold) 9 (hold) 12 (hold) 15 (hold)18 (hold) 21 (hold) 24 (hold) 27 (hold) 30 (hold). Ready to give it a try? Let's all do it together and say the numbers out loud with a big strong voice, 3 (hold) 6 (hold) 9 (hold) 12 (hold) 15 (hold)18 (hold) 21 (hold) 24 (hold) 27 (hold) 30 (hold). Good work! You are really getting the hang of this; pretty soon you'll be teaching other kids."

▶ **VIDEO 11: Slowing down to learn.**

"We can learn our spelling words, state capitals, vocabulary definitions – shoot, we can even learn Latin, Spanish or French! Let's experiment – who has something they want us to learn in half notes? We'll do it as a group, together."

"When we learn something new, we do it in the slow, slow or half note beat. This way, we have time to learn or encode the new information. Beats help us learn. Movement helps us learn and how fast we move calls upon different types of memory, quarter notes for retrieval and half notes for encoding or learning. Now, we can play with learning using musical rhythm."

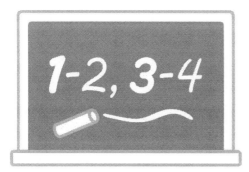
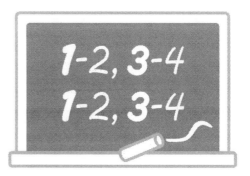

Activity #5

Musical Thinking - Motor Exploration
THINKING IN WHOLE NOTES

"You know how sometimes a teacher or your parent asks you a question like, 'What was the theme of this book chapter?' or 'Where do you want to go for Spring Break?' You have an answer and you wish to share it, but you need a moment to think about it. The answer isn't on the tip of your tongue. In Musical Thinking, we have a way for you to say, 'Hold on a sec, I am thinking about it,' without saying a word."

"What we do is, we communicate in a whole note. A whole note is four beats, so it gives us time to think. If you step or march a whole note, what does it look like? That's right it's 1 x x x. We can communicate that we'd like a second to think about it by holding our fists up in front of our bodies horizontally to say, 'Wait, a moment, I'm thinking about the answer.' This is a terrific strategy for when you want to answer but you need a few seconds. Let's try it."

"If we are a class of students or even just a single student talking with a parent or teacher and the adult asks, 'What does infinity mean?' and we have the answer in the back of our minds, but we need a moment to retrieve the answer and then say it, we can put up our fists horizontally in front of our bodies to say, 'Hold on a sec, I'm thinking. I'll be with you in a moment when I have the answer.' Let's try it. We can pair up and ask one another questions that take a moment to respond to. One person can be the 'asker' and the other can be the 'responder.' Stand across from your partner and try it. Ask a question and let the responder 'think is a whole note telling you with their hands, 'hold on I am thinking about that.' Then when the responder has the answer, they can say it."

"What happens if you think about the answer and then realize you can't recall it or do not know it? No worries, just open your first fingers on your fists, your pointer fingers and point to the 'asker.' Your pointer fingers tell the 'asker,' 'I thought about it and I can't answer that right now, you are 'released' to go on to the next person.'"

"In our pairs, let's try thinking and communicating in whole notes and then talk with one another about what we experienced and what we noticed."

 VIDEO 12: Hold on I'm Thinking.

Musical Thinking – Motor Exploration
SOMETIMES YOU GOTTA REST

"You guys have done such a great job! I have one more note to play with you and that is the rest note. The rest note tells us to pause and take a rest. It is accompanied by silence." "Let's all try to be totally silent for a moment, when I say 'Go, we will all be silent together. Ready Set 'Go!'"

The class is then quiet. The teacher might nod her head to show how long they will be quiet. When she nods her head four times, they are being silent for one measure. "Pretty cool, eh, we can be silent for a specific amount of time, in this case, we were silent for one measure. Now there is actually a sign musical conductors could use to tell the musicians we are being silent now, we are resting."

The teacher then lifts her hands like a conductor and places both her hands open and laying flat, together, in front of her body at about heart level. Think about when yoga teachers say "Namaste," their hands are pressed together, palms touching and fingers pointing upwards, thumbs close to the chest. That's the movement we do to show we are resting.

We call this position "The Peaceful Heart." I have said to many a child, "Let's return to our peaceful hearts," which tells the children "Let's rest for a moment, quietly, so that our brains and bodies can relax."

The teacher or clinician can now practice with the class, by asking the class to show her their 'peaceful heart' position. "Let's all return to our peaceful hearts. You all try it, place your palms pressed together at heart level like this. Remember, we did a closed fist sign to show we were thinking. Well, it's similar here, but our hands are in front of our hearts. We are using a sign here as well, but now we are simply saying, 'Let's be peaceful and rest'."

Activity #7

Musical Thinking – Motor Exploration
WALKING IN QUARTER NOTES

Walking in Quarter Notes is a fine way to engage with students as they walk to your office or to an activity. What Walking in Quarter Notes reminds me of is learning how to do the steps in jazz dance class, which I was never able to do. I think if somebody had shown me that you can walk, move, stomp, clap or even do a pirouette in eighth notes, quarter notes or half notes, the complicated dance sequences would have been easier to learn.

Essentially, you learn new steps in half notes and once you understand them, you perform them in quarter notes, or even eighth notes. Using Musical Thinking, we show children that natural rhythms and beats apply so much to how we move in everyday life, that we are empowered to make choices about the speed at which we move and how we express ourselves.

Walking in Quarter Notes is often the first activity I ever do with a child when I am introducing Musical Thinking. It's a simple, uncomplicated, non-threatening way to suggest that rhythm matters, without being intellectual about it. "Walk with me." "Hey, we are walking in quarter notes can you hear it?" It's a really soft beginning. All you do is walk, maybe count, laugh, smile, join the student's pace and maybe even slow down for a few steps to explore what that feels like. Then move on to whatever else you had planned. The child has had a brief introduction to Musical Thinking and you can delve deeper when the time is right.

Musical Thinking – Motor Exploration
MEET THE LOVE NOTES

Science tells us that labeling and categorizing concepts helps the brain manage information in a more organized manner. Therefore, we have names for each of the four musical notes to facilitate communication and learning. We usually teach the children how to walk, step, march or clap in quarter notes and half notes, then we teach them how to move or count beats in whole notes. We teach them the hand sign for "I am thinking," and we show them the hand sign for 'We are resting' or 'I am storing.'" These are four simple notes and two hand gestures that open up a new world of thinking and communication.

Next, and perhaps best of all, we tell them, "Our notes have names. Our notes are like a musical quartet. We call the quartet 'The Love Notes.' Let me introduce you to each note as we march our beats and you can see how they can help you in all sorts of ways."

The teacher lifts up the Musical Thinking cards or projects them on the smart board, marker board or chalkboard. You have a lot of leeway here. You can introduce one note at a time, or you can introduce all the notes in the entire quartet picture. You can ask a child in the group, class or family to stand up and march, clap, step, or walk one of the notes and then introduce the note by name, whatever suits your client, group, class or family. Allow me to introduce the members of the Musical Thinking Quartet to you and then you can take it away.

THINKERBELLE

Thinkerbelle is a whole note. She represents one beat for four counts. Thinkerbelle is associated with thinking. When the children wish to take a bit of time to think something out, they rely on Thinkerbelle.

SLOW MO

Slow Mo is a half note. He represents two counts in a four beat measure, 1-2, 3-4. Slow Mo moves at around 50 beats per minute and is associated with encoding. When the children are taking the content, knowledge or information into their brains, they rely on Slow Mo.

BESS REST

Bess Rest is the rest note. Bess Rest represents a pause in the music; she can also represent the end of a musical sequence. In real music, there are all sorts of rest notes; we use the quarter note rest for all of our teaching because this is Musical Thinking, not music class (smile). The children rely on Bess Rest when they are storing information in their memories.

QUICK RICK

Quick Rick is a quarter note. He represents four beats per measure, 1-2-3-4. Quick Rick is the fastest of the four notes. Quick Rick moves at about 85 beats per minute. This is not exactly twice as fast as Slow Mo, but it is a nice pace for recalling stored information. When children have learned information and they can recall it rather quickly, they rely on Quick Rick.

Clearly, when children are able to access information very rapidly, they can do so in an eighth note, twice as fast as Quick Rick. We do not name this note, but we can play games that show how fast well-stored information can be recalled. All we need to do is play and use our imaginations. As an example, many children are able to count by 10's very quickly. Sometimes, particularly when we use Musical Thinking to teach and practice skip counting, we show them that well-stored information, which is highly automated, can be recalled super fast, as in eighth notes.

We use the The Love Notes or The Musical Thinking Quartet in so many ways, their limit is simply a matter of creativity and imagination on the part of clinicians, teachers and, most of all, students.

The Love Notes

MARY AND HER "ME, ME, ME'S"

Here's another sweet story that shows us how a school psychologist helped a child using Musical Thinking.

Mary is an enthusiastic 11-year-old student. When her teacher asks a question in class, Mary excitedly throws her arm in the air with her fingers wiggling, as if to say, "Me, me, me, over here, I've got the answer." Mary doesn't see that the other kids in class are annoyed by her constant requests for attention. She is loud and the other children would like her to be less enthusiastic and more quiet. Mary has been prompted by the teacher several times to offer to answer a question just a few times in class each day so that other children can have a chance answering. But Mary remains undeterred, as she is really excited about answering questions.

One day the teacher asks the school psychologist how to help Mary inhibit her behavior better. In under ten minutes, the clinician introduces Mary to Musical Thinking, and Mary is able to voluntarily shift her behavior to a calmer more controlled state. This is how the conversation went.

SP: "Hi, Mary, I'm Mrs. Comizio. it's so great to have you visit me today."

M: "Hey, do you have any toys?"

SP: "I sure do and you are welcome to play with them. Let me show you some toys now." "Here we have some musical notes."

M: "Oh, they have names!"

SP: "That's right. We have Slow Mo, Quick Rick, Thinkerbelle and Bess Rest. Funny thing is, these musical notes enjoy games like How Fast Do I Raise My Hand. Would you like to play?"

M: "Sure, I love games."

SP: "Alright then, you hold our musical notes, which we call The Love Notes."

M: "Oh, they are cute."

SP: "So let's meet them. Quick Rick moves really fast, Slow Mo moves nice and slow, Thinkerbelle stops and thinks for a few seconds and Bess Rest encourages everyone to take a breather."

M: "I like Thinkerbelle best."

SP: "Great, I'll give you a Thinkerbelle sticker when it's time to return to class."

M: "I love her."

SP: "So, you know when your teacher asks a question in class?"

M: "Yeah, she does that all day."

SP: "What do you do when Mrs. Bales asks a question?"

M:	"Oh, I raise my hand."

SP:	"Show me what it looks like when you raise your hand."

M:	"I do this!" (Mary raises her hand and waves it, moving her entire body, while leaning forward.)

SP:	"Oh, so you raise your hand like Quick Rick on a bucking bronco." Mary laughs.

M:	"Yeah, cause I want Mrs. Bales to call on me."

SP:	"Did you know that Mrs. Bales usually calls on the students who are raising their hand like Slow Mo and holding it quietly in the air like Thinkerbelle?"

M:	"Let me think, no."

SP:	"You think, exactly, just like Thinkerbelle. We can actually raise our hands in class using The Love Notes, do you wanna try?"

M:	"As long as I can be Thinkerbelle."

SP:	"You sure can. First, let's raise our hands like Quick Rick on a bucking bronco."

	They both raise one hand and wave it noisily.

SP:	"Wow, he's kinda noisy, eh?"

SP:	"I wonder if he may annoy the other kids?"

SP:	"Now let's raise our hand like Slow Mo and hold it quietly like Thinkerbelle."

	They each raise a hand as Mrs. Comizio counts slowly, 1 and 2 and. Then, as they hold their hands in the air, Mrs. Comizio says 1 and nods her head slowly for counts 2, 3, 4. Mrs. Comizio smiles.

SP:	"Now that we are raising our hand like Slow Mo and holding it quietly like Thinkerbelle, we can imagine Thinkerbelle thinking, 'I'll hold my hand up here quietly for a few more counts and if Mrs. Bales doesn't call on me, I'll lower my hand and rest with Bess Rest. Then I'll wait quietly for the next time I can slowly raise my hand.'"

M:	"You mean Thinkerbelle thinks?"

SP:	"When we use our imagination, we can imagine she does. See, The Love Notes are here to help children in many ways. One way is to help them count the beats in order to move more slowly, quietly and calmly. Let's use The Love Notes again and this time you can quietly do the counting."

	They practice again and then make a plan for Mary to teach her class about how The Love Notes can help the children do all sorts of things.

Musical Thinking – Motor Exploration
MUSICAL THINKING AND EVERYDAY LIFE

The introduction of the concept that we can move, count, read, and behave in quarter notes and half notes is usually astounding to the children. The fact that the notes have names facilitates a broad range of verbal and gestural communication.

Now, the teacher can use Musical Thinking to encourage conversation, asking the class what kinds of activities we typically do in quarter notes, and what kinds of activities we typically do in half notes. At this point, the children might respond that we walk to the drinking fountain in quarter notes, but we get our supplies out of our backpacks in half notes.

Once the children are beginning to understand that we can assign the rate of speed of our movement to musical notes, the implications are enormous. As an example, we could ask the entire class to raise their hands in half notes, and then hold their hands up for a whole note, as we saw in the story "Mary and her Me Me Me's." The teacher can provide cuing to the students by counting as the children raise their hands in a half note, 1, 2 and then hold their hands in the air as a whole note, 1, 2, 3, 4.

So now we can talk to the class about the fact that if a student can retrieve academic information in quarter notes, that shows us that they have learned the information, and it is actually stored in their memory. If the child is still learning the material, they might be moving or thinking in half notes, when the brain is encoding the new information.

Being playful and engaging the class in conversation around what kinds of activities they do in different notes can even bring laughter to the classroom. As an example, the teacher can ask the students what types of activities they can do in eighth notes. "Do we brush our teeth in eighth notes or half notes? Do we run down the stairs in eighth notes or half notes? Do we eat our dinner in eighth notes or half notes? Let's explore how we think, feel and behave with Musical Thinking."

It is also true that we can manage our feelings, movements and self-regulation by responding in half notes, quarter notes or whole notes. As an example, if a child is talking with his teacher about not understanding the meaning of a vocabulary word or the instructions for a history project, he might be tempted to communicate quickly, perhaps even loudly, but the best way for the teacher to hear him in order to help him is if he speaks calmly in half notes, so the teacher can hear his concerns and respond to him appropriately. Musical Thinking helps us not only think and learn, but to express our thoughts and behaviors in a more pro-social manner.

Musical Thinking Musical Compositions

Simply by introducing The Love Notes and moving to different beats in a variety of sequences, you have been creating musical compositions. You have marched, stepped, tapped and moved in quarter notes, half-notes, whole notes and rest. The children with whom you work might have even danced, and once they get moving they are energized to learn and create.

The Musical Composition section of Musical Thinking helps the children experience how truly creative they are. Now, as a class or individually with the children in the clinical hour, you can write and even perform your own compositions. We shall start with some easy compositions and then move on to create entire orchestras within your class, family or clinical group.

Let's begin by understanding that in Musical Thinking we can "feel the music" with Motor Exploration. We can write and even "be" the music with "Musical Compositions." We can use The Love Notes and all that we have learned about tempo, rhythm and timing to be empowered to think and learn in a new way.

Next, we will explore Musical Compositions, and how to create and write musical sequences in three cognitively engaging ways:

1. Applying The Love Notes in their learning.

2. Using letter abbreviations for The Love Notes – W H R and Q – as another way to compose pieces of cognitive-motor movement.

3. Use slow and quick notes to learn academic and behavioral content.

If you have been playing Musical Thinking with the children in your class or practice, they are likely already creating compositions. Children are creative, and once they begin to experience what quick notes and slow notes feel like, they naturally begin to create combinations. It's a natural evolution of their learning to scaffold up and make their own movements a bit more challenging. Over many hours of walking, marching, stomping, clapping, hopping, running and more, the children taught me to become more creative in the applications of Musical Thinking to both their learning and behavior. As the play progressed, some children wanted simple sequenced progressions of steps and movements, whereas others wanted complicated progressions. What follows are some of the Musical Thinking Compositions that evolved. There are many possible variations on the activities. Let your imagination and your interactions with the children be your guide.

Let's Get Started with
THE TWO-STEP!

The Love Notes Abbreviations

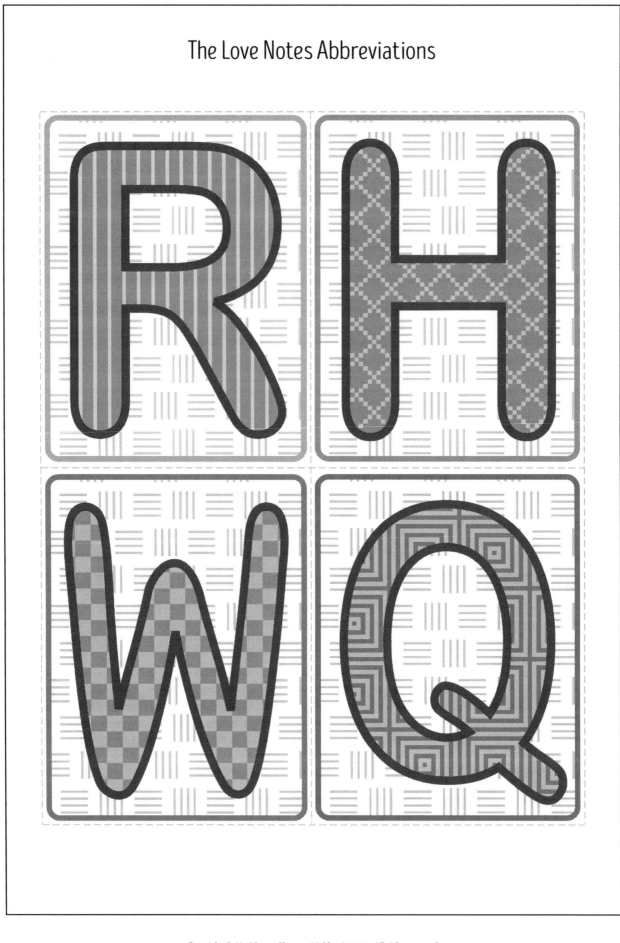

Activity #1

Musical Thinking – Composition
THE TWO-STEP

"Let's get our groove on, kids! In Musical Thinking, we can dance. I'll teach you the two-step, then maybe you can teach me some hip hop."

"Let's all line up facing the front of the room. So we'll begin with our right foot and we'll take one step, then one step with our left foot, then one with our right foot. So, it's super simple, three small steps, right, left, right. The fun is in how we add The Love Notes. So now, we'll stand with our feet together and do that again, walk right, left, right. Now we will picture Quick Rick and Slow Mo and we'll step on our right foot, quick, then our left foot, quick, then our right foot, slow. Ready – Quick, Quick, Slow. Excellent! So now we can stand in a line, a circle or a square; we can even stand across from one another and mirror our feet by having one person start on their right foot and the other start on their left. You got it! Practice, play, make combinations with twirls or shimmys. That's The Two-Step – Quick Quick Slow."

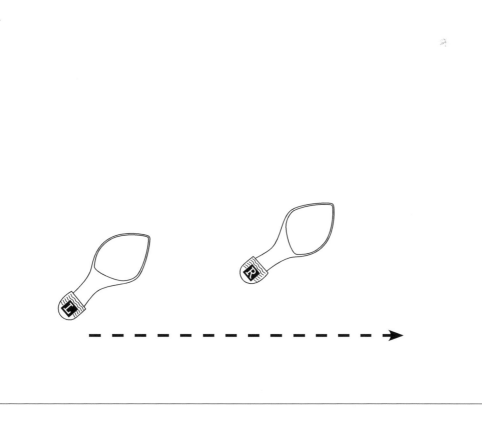

Musical Thinking - Composition
THE LITTLE JANE FONDA

"Have you ever been in a Zumba class? You know how you do different dance steps to the music. Well, in The Little Jane Fonda, we choose an energetic song and we choose two different motor moves such as side step and heels up. Then we do each move for eight counts, then four counts, then two counts, then one count. This is a great way to wake up our brains and bodies so that we are alert and ready to learn."

* "Let's try it. We are all in ready position.

* Now we step side to side right foot then left foot for 8-7-6-5-4-3-2-1, now heels up 8-7-6-5-4-3-2-1. Let's put that together.

* Side step 8-7-6-5-4-3-2-1, heels up 8-7-6-5-4-3-2-1. Excellent.

* Now we'll do each move for four beats. Side step 4-3-2-1, now heels up 4-3-2-1, again, side step 4-3-2-1, now heels up 4-3-2-1.

* Now we'll do twos, you all ready? Breathe deeply, your energy is soaring!

* Side step 2-1, heels up 2-1, again side step 2-1, heels up 2-1, again side step 2-1, heels up 2-1, last time side step 2-1, heels up 2-1.

* Now we will step side, heel up, for eight counts.

* Mix and match your steps, simply moving in measures and notes. You can add some arm movements as well. It's super energizing and fun!"

See the list of movement ideas at the end of this chapter. They will inspire you to make up your own sets or sequences.

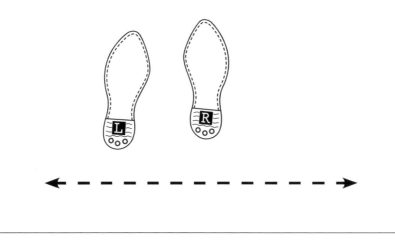

Musical Thinking - Composition
THE MUSICAL THINKING ORCHESTRA

 VIDEO 13: The MT Orchestra.

Research speaks to the value of music and rhythm as a social connector. When we move, step, tap, march and make noise together, we feel more cohesive. We can turn the class (client, family or group) into an orchestra, creating a meaningful group experience, by telling them that we are going to step or march in a series of notes for four measures. You can define the notes with ease simply using Quick Rick or Slow Mo in any combination. Start out simple, perhaps four beats of Quick Rick, then four beats of Slow Mo, then mix them up. Change the tempo or add a movement, such as hands to the sky, for one beat. Can you feel it? 1-2-3-4 1 x 3 hands up then down!

As you all become more familiar with writing compositions, the class (client, family or group) can perform their own music. We can draw it on the board or on a piece of paper. We plan it out, we practice it and then we perform it. You are an orchestra!

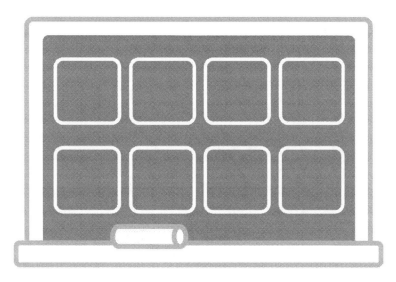

There are endless hours of creative fun with this activity as the children, families, classrooms, even staff can play with the four musical notes, writing measures of music and then stepping them out. Eventually, you can tap, clap, stomp, shimmy, dance, etc. You can even add different motor movements to each note and be a full body orchestra!

Activity #4

Musical Thinking – Composition
WE ARE COMPOSERS!

▶ **VIDEO 14: MT Compositions.**

So far, we have explored the graphic representations of notes and we have named them. We have marched to different tempos, and added some gross motor movements or sounds when we desire. Now we wish to explore more about written compositions in Musical Thinking. How much fun do you think it is, particularly for students who have any difficulty learning, to begin to experience themselves as musical composers?

Intuition tells us that we can understand Thinkerbelle to be T, Slow Mo to be S, Quick Rick to be Q and Bess Rest to be B. Simple, eh? But if you have some BIG thinkers in your classroom, they might wish to compose in reference to the type of note, not the name of the note. Perhaps they have taken music before and they have an idea of the symbol for a quarter note or a half note. They might even be totally new to music, yet thinking in notes is helpful to them.

In this case, we have another way to communicate using Musical Thinking. We can label Thinkerbelle W for a whole note. Slow Mo is H for a half note. Quick Rick is Q for a quarter note and Bess Rest is R for rest. If you are in a music class, you can write music with notes on a staff. In Musical Thinking you can write measures of thinking, learning or behavior with four letters. How cool is that! Wait until the children with whom you work come into your classroom or office with written orchestrations; you will be amazed and delighted.

Remember in the composition activities 1–4 when we were teaching the children how to march, step or walk in quarter notes, half notes, whole notes and a rest note? Let's play a game here, where we compose some Musical Thinking 'music.' You don't even need a staff. All you need is a pen, pencil, marker or piece of chalk. Write out one measure of notes. It might look like Q-Q-Q-Q. That would be four quarter notes in one measure. Let's replace a quarter note with a half note. You can use an x to show that you are holding a beat.

What would that look like? It could be Q-Q-H-x, or Q-H-x-Q or H-x-Q-Q. And the beat goes on . . . . It's all up to you and the beautiful children with whom you work.

Shall we step up our game and write two measures? Continue to use just Slow Mo and Quick Rick, the half note and the quarter note. Try it – take out a piece of paper and write out eight beats, that's four beats per measure. On the following page there are some boxes to help you out. Tap out the notes as you write them down, if a little cuing helps you.

There are so many fun combinations you might have written; for example,

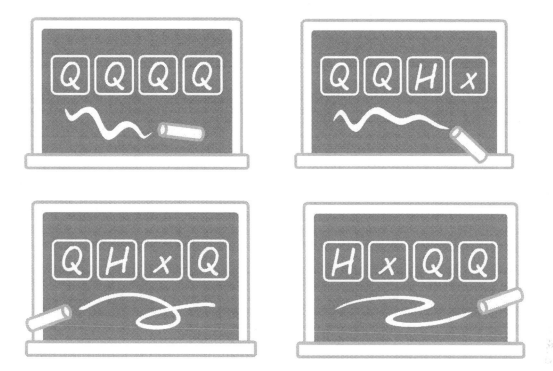

I hope you are having so much fun now that you are writing a symphony. Before we move on, write four measures and add Thinkerbelle and Bess Rest, the whole note and the rest note. In all the time I have played Musical Thinking with clinicians, teachers and students, I have only started or concluded a musical thinking activity with Bess Rest. She is the sign for my students that the activity is completed and we are moving on. You might be more creative than I and find a way to use her in new ways, let your brain wander and ponder.

Here you go, four measures – give it a try.

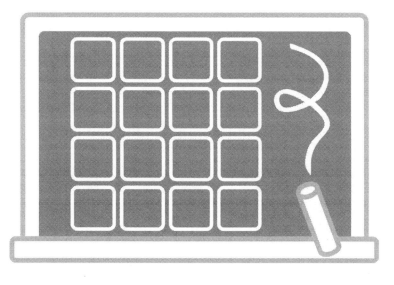

Musical Thinking - Composition
WALKING COMPOSITIONS

Now that the children have learned measures, we could walk in circles, walk in serpentines, walk around the tennis court, walk on the basketball court. You could walk in your driveway. You can make patterns just in your backyard. And all you do is take your musical thinking staff and write out what notes you are going to do.

Let's say you are going to do Q, Q, Q, Q, H, H, Q, Q, Q, Q, H, H. So you'd be doing four measures. One measure of quarter notes, one measure of half notes, a measure of quarter notes and a measure of half notes. Very simple. Okay.

It's very fun for the children to experience what this actually feels like when they Step, Step, Step, Step; Step Hold, Step Hold; Step, Step, Step, Step; Step Hold, Step Hold. So there they are. Walking in the Qs and Hs or quarter notes and half notes or the quick, quick, slow, slow. And you can make all sorts of patterns, just walking. We call it walking compositions. Now the client, student, class, group or family can write a composition together, practice it and even make it more complex by walking in circles, figure eights or serpentines.

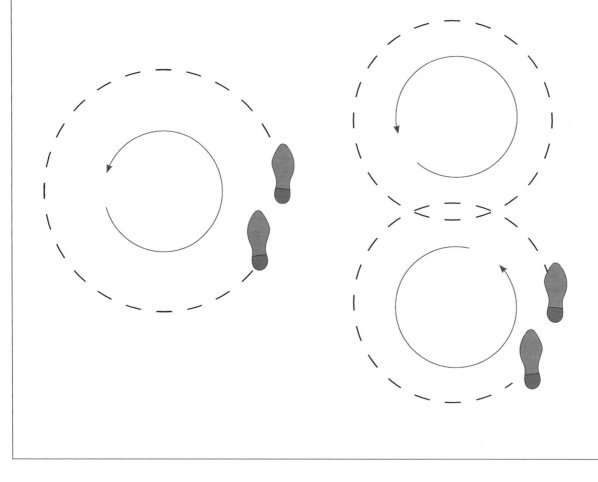

Musical Thinking - Composition
MUSICAL MOVEMENT COMPOSITIONS

Now that the children are getting the hang of Musical Thinking, they can increase the motor complexity by adding a wide range of motor movements to the notes. They could write a two- to four-measure composition and add motor movements. As an example, every time they do a quarter note, they could jump, and every time they do a half note, they could clap. This could be done with marching or in place of marching. We have added everything from vocal sounds to complex motor movements like crab walks when we wrote and performed "Musical Compositions" with children. For the super fast thinkers, you might even add cognitive elements over the compositions to learn vocabulary, spelling, Latin, French, history, science and more.

Consider some of these moves (and sounds), or make up your own.

MOVEMENT AND SOUND IDEAS FOR MUSICAL THINKING ACTIVITIES

Airplane	Crab walk	Plank	Stomp
Angel arms	Giraffe walk	Push-up	Superman
Arms out to the side	Heel walk	Shimmy	Tap
	Helicopter	Shout	Tiger crawl
Arms straight up	High knees	Shuffle	Tiptoe walk
Balance on one leg	Hips side to side	Skip	Toe touches
Change direction (backward, to the side, in a square, etc.)	Hop	Snap	Yoga poses
	Jump	Sounds: Bark, click, growl, honk, meow	
Clap	Monster walk		

Generally, as we orchestrate Musical Thinking compositions, we add five possible layers – the note, a sound, a fine motor movement, a gross motor movement or a cue such as counting out the beats – as we transition from one note to the next. Once we have the beat, sounds and movements down, we can layer cognition, knowledge or learning on top. The combinations are endless.

A Whole New Way To Learn and Communicate

When we take a moment to think about it, Musical Thinking is an exciting communication medium. A child can think in visual images as they picture The Love Notes. They can think in rhythm as the notes represent beats per minute. They can use the two primary Musical Thinking gestures, the "Peaceful Heart" position and Thinkerbelle's "I'm Thinking" hand gesture, to communicate nonverbally. They can even write Musical Thinking out in numbers such as 1-2; 3-4. There is one more evolution of Musical Thinking communication I wish to share with you. Once children have been introduced to the rhythm, beats, graphical pictures, note names, and letters, we show them that they can layer cognition on top of tempo, rhythm and timing to learn academic, behavioral or social knowledge.

Musical Thinking: More Cognitive Applications - Cognitive Cuing

We apply Musical Thinking to so many aspects of learning and behavior. You can use The Love Notes as well as the rhythmic movement to do almost anything. We have taught children how to sit at the dining room table in eight measures of Thinkerbelle. We have shown children how to carry heavy boxes downstairs in Slow Mo. Once, an older sibling taught his younger brother how to build a tower of Legos, while remaining calm, with The Love Notes. We have even helped children learn their history facts! On the next page, is a short story from our colorful Musical Thinking Quick Start Manual, *Musical Thinking: Steps to Teaching Children How They Think* (Kenney, 2016).

One of the unique aspects of Musical Thinking Cognitive Applications is that we provide direct instruction to the children regarding their executive functions with cueing cards. This way, as we are working on academic, learning, behavioral, social, emotional or self-regulation skills, we empower the children to be more knowing about what skills they are using and what skills they wish to use more of or improve.

We cue by asking the children to:

- Define the task.
- Name one or two executive function skills needed to execute the task.
- Define the relevant cognitive skill (in their own words).
- Tell what they are going to do to engage the skill to execute the task.

Then we review with the child what worked and what they'd like to do differently next time.

The following are a few different types of cuing examples.

SARAH, SIR ISAAC NEWTON AND MUSICAL THINKING

SPOTLIGHT STORY

Sarah has to study a page of biographical facts for an upcoming test. In the past, she has rushed through her studying without taking many notes, color coding information or making flash cards. Today, her father is trying to help her develop a strategy for transferring the factual information to color-coded flash cards so that she can remember the facts with a more thorough study system.

D: "Sarah, let's use Musical Thinking to study our facts about Isaac Newton. Can you tell me a bit about Isaac Newton?"

S: "You know, dad, he was a scientist."

D: "Oh, yes, I remember, now when did he live?"

S: "I don't know, look at the book."

D: "What a great idea! How about you take out a note card, label it and write down relevant facts about Isaac Newton. I see some facts right here in the book. We need to read one fact at a time and make flash cards from this paragraph."

Sir Isaac Newton, PRS, MP, was born December 25, 1642 and died March 20, 1727. Newton was a physicist and mathematician from England. He was known as a "natural philosopher" in his day. Newton was one of the most influential scientists in history. Sir Isaac Newton is best known for his theories on gravity. Alongside Gottfried Leibniz, Newton is credited with the development of calculus.

S: "Hurry up, dad, iCarly is on soon."

D: "Since we are learning new information, how could Slow Mo help us?"

S: "Slow-Mo would say take your time, write it down and say it out loud."

D: "There we go, that's a great strategy, let's open the book, read the facts, write them down and say them out loud. If Slow Mo is helping us, what would slowing down sound like?"

Sarah taps on her desk with her hands and her dad passes her a pencil and they play around for a moment tapping out slow beats. Now Sarah is smiling.

D: "Let's 'Slow Mo' this paragraph in order to separate each fact, write it down, color code it and then say it out loud. By the time we are done, iCarly will be on."

In this short passage, Sarah's father has engaged her with humor and music. He has spoken with her about some of the underlying skills demonstrated by several executive functions including alerting, selecting, pacing, planning, inhibiting and organizing. He has even made one of The Love Notes a verb. Sarah's father said, "Let's Slow-Mo this." To Sarah that now means let's slow this down, take it one step at a time and complete each part of the task sequentially.

Now they can take out the note cards and colored pens and begin to write down some of the Isaac Newton facts in a well-categorized, color-coded manner. The very act of first reading the paragraph, then writing down each individual fact on a notecard has started the learning process. Each cognitive interaction with the content increases the ability of the child to encode and store the information.

SPOTLIGHT STORY

A COGNITIVE CONVERSATION WITH JOEY ABOUT HIS APPROACH TO LEARNING HIS VOCABULARY WORDS

Joey is studying his vocabulary words.

a. **CUING INTRODUCTION**

    i.   The clinician or teacher: "Joey, we're going to study your vocabulary words now. Let's think for a moment, what are some cognitive skills your brain will need to study your vocabulary words?"

    ii. Joey: "I need to sequence this task. I am going to write the first five vocabulary words each on a separate index card. Then I will place them in a deck in front of me. I will turn one card over at a time and first I will say the word, then I will spell the word, then I will define the word.

b. **MUSICAL THINKING COGNITIVE APPLICATION** - At this point, Joey knows a lot about Musical Thinking. He understands rhythm, tempo and timing. He has met The Love Notes and has created compositions. Now he is ready to choose a specific Musical Thinking note or sequence on which he will layer his vocabulary words, so that he may practice the vocabulary words one at a time using rhythmic movement.

    i.   The clinician or teacher: "That sounds great. What Musical Thinking tool will you use to reinforce your learning?"

    ii. Joey: "Since these are new words this week, I will march out each word in Slow Mo first. I might even take my time if a word is hard and use Thinkerbelle. When I feel the word is encoded, I'll retrieve it with Quick Rick."

c. **ADDITIONAL CUING QUESTIONS** - What supplies will you need? What will you do first? What will you do in what order? How will you chunk this task? How will you know when you have learned a word? When will you know this task is done? How will you signal to me that you want me to join you in the marching or counting? How will you signal to me that you want my help with a word?

SPOTLIGHT STORY

JANNELLE AND HER "OH SO BORING" VOCABULARY WORDS

Jannelle is a third grader who is beginning to take weekly vocabulary tests. This means that every week on Monday, Jannelle gets a new list of vocabulary words; she needs to memorize them by Friday, the day on which she has the test. The first week, Jannelle was excited by this new task. But now she is in Week 5 and her reluctance to study is causing conflict in her family.

After her mom learned about Musical Thinking, she felt empowered to approach this arduous task of weekly memorization from a musical perspective.

After school, Jannelle's mother goes into the living room on her own and starts marching, moving and dancing in simple measure of quarter notes and half notes. She does so slowly and melodically to the point where she is actually enjoying herself. Jannelle runs down the stairs and stops abruptly to look at her mom "being weird" in the living room.

J: "Mom, you are so embarrassing."

M: "I'm practicing vocabulary."

J: "You are double weird, mom."

M: "I have a lot to hold in my working memory right now."

J: "That's right, Mom, you are encoding your words, move slowly to really learn them."

M: "So I step like Slow Mo as I think of the vocabulary word. What are the words on your list?"

J: "Let's see, they are concentrate, conclude, demonstrate, distract, flexible, focus, generosity, master, outstanding, routine."

M: "Okay, so let me think about this, if I want to step out CONCENTRATE, how many syllables do we have? CON-CEN-TRATE, we have three! I can do this! I'll go half note, half note, half note, then I'll clap, like Bess Rest, to say "We've done it!" So it will be one word, three syllables in two measures. Oh, this is fun! Wanna try it with me?"

When you get to the cognitive applications tool in Musical Thinking, these conversations come naturally. You and the child have developed a new communication tool and the child is excited to practice, use and even teach you his skills. So trust your clinical intuition; this is a conversation, not a script.

Sometimes we even make cuing cards with the children. Where they write the cognitive skill or executive function, they define it, then they write an example of when they commonly use that skill. You can see that you are encouraging the application of metacognition, as well as thinking skills at the same time. The child is observing the process of how he thinks, while he thinks. It's pretty darn cool to see the children flourish.

Here is another approach to vocabulary words, one that includes cuing.

A Few More Cognitive Comments

Let's look now at how we use Musical Thinking for memorization. Even if we only have twenty minutes with a child one time, we can introduce tempo through Quick Rick and Slow Mo and literally change how a child thinks. Curiously, I just did this last weekend with my daughter at tennis. The tempo on her serve was in 4/4 time, pretty fast. Quick, Quick, Quick, Quick. Yet her coach told her it needed to be 1-2-3, not 1-2-3-4. So when I said to her, "It's more like Slow Slow Quick," she felt it right away. That's how easy it is to simply say to anyone, "Go slow, then quick." Everyone from 5-year-olds to 80-year-olds get it, fast.

Okay, back to memorization. As we have said, the way we apply The Love Notes to cognitive learning is we simply introduce new material in Slow Mo, often initially with a 50 bpm song or a metronome. We also initially retrieve it in Slow Mo, because we are learning novel content. Then, as the child gets a better grasp on the material, we ask the child to retrieve the content in Quick Rick. We do this for social skills, foreign language, spelling words, math facts and more.

Before we move on, let me provide you with an example of how you can teach social skills with The Love Notes. Imagine you are working with Jennifer, who is on the autism spectrum. She wants to learn how to greet an important adult who will be visiting her school. Once Jennifer is introduced to The Love Notes, you can use them to walk through a task, such as how to shake someone's hand.

You simply establish marching or walking to the beat with the child and then walk her through the handshake process. "First we use Thinkerbelle to imagine what we will do when we shake Mrs. Swenson's hand. Then we reach out in three slow counts. Ready? Let's try – hand out, shake, hand down to your side." "Excellent! Let's try it again; we'll do it in Slow Mo, so our movement is smooth and natural." "Great work! What else can we practice using The Love Notes?"

You can use Musical Thinking for so many aspects of skills improvement. The sky is the limit! Most of all, partner with the children, be creative and have fun! We hope you enjoy learning, dancing, clapping, counting, marching and more; now let's move ahead to some executive function activity ideas. Here is a story to help us remember the learning is all about relationships.

SPOTLIGHT STORY

CONNECTING IS WHAT COUNTS

The other day, I met a first-grade class outside to pick up a student for a counseling appointment. I had arranged this time with his teacher and did not realize that I would be taking him away from recess. It was a simply perfect early fall day. When the teacher called him over, Johnny was visibly upset. Shoulders slumped, frown on his face and a loud whine emanating from his lips. The teacher said, "What's that about?" and Johnny said, "Because I was having a good time playing and you called me over and now I have to leave." The teacher explained that the students were just about to get called over to line up and go inside as well, but this did not comfort Johnny at all. He and I walked down the hall while he was loudly telling me, "This is the WORST!"

When we got to my office and sat down, I tried to reflect back what Johnny was feeling. I said, "I get it. You were outside having a great time and you are upset that you had to cut it short, even if it was just a couple of minutes short. You weren't expecting that. I'm glad you are here, though; I thought we could have a nice meeting." Johnny didn't soften, "Yeah! That is right. I don't want to have a nice meeting!" he exclaimed. I just nodded and waited. Next, he caught a glimpse of the card game, Uno, sitting on my shelf. "Oh, I know Uno!" he said. I asked, "Would you like to play while we talk?" He nodded. I asked him to remind me of the rules and as he did, his voice lightened and lifted and he smiled. While we played our game, I said, "I want to show you something…" and I began to draw. I drew stick figure pictures, explaining that I am still a working-on-it artist.

The first picture was a little boy holding a lunch box with a circle mouth standing next to a tall teacher with a straight line mouth. Then I drew myself, a stick figure with a triangle skirt and a small smile mouth next to the boy with the circle mouth in the hallway, and finally the two of us sitting in chairs but now the boy had a smile mouth too. I pointed to the first picture, "Do you know who this represents?" "Me?" he asked. "Yes," I said. "That is you outside with a round mouth because you are mad and you are talking with a mad voice. This is you in the hallway with me. I am not mad, I'm happy to be seeing you today, but you are still mad in the hallway. Now look at us here - this is still you, but what changed?" Johnny said, "I'm happy now." "That's right," I said, "But the thing that you were mad about, leaving recess didn't change, right? So what changed for you that you are happy now?"

Johnny furrowed his brow and thought for a moment. I offered, "When you had the circle mouth, what were you saying?" Johnny said, "I don't want to go inside, and in the hallway I was saying, this was the worst time and I didn't want to be going with you." "Yes, that's right. I remember. What were you saying here in the chair?" Johnny thought, "I was talking about Uno." Then I said, "Ah, so the words you were saying out loud were different … and it looks like you were also feeling different when those words changed to something that you liked. What were the words that you were saying in your head when you sat down here?" "Well, I saw your Uno game and I was thinking, I love Uno and I'm good at it!" I said, "Do you see what a wonderful thing you did today, Johnny? You bossed back the words that made you feel bad, and you found words to say that made you feel glad and calm and even happy. The situation didn't change, but you changed so that you could make the best of it and you didn't let a small bad thing turn into a long bad day. I am so proud of you!" Johnny beamed! I beamed! And we played Uno and he won, fair and square.

Thinking Activities for Better Executive Function

chapter 4

The activities in Chapter 4 are age-appropriate ways we have played with children in our offices and schools to help enhance components of executive function and thinking skills. These are clinically chosen activities that allow children to practice their executive function skills. They represent a sample of the many activities that can support healthy thinking skill development. Enjoy them, change them, improve them, model them and best of all - **PLAY!**

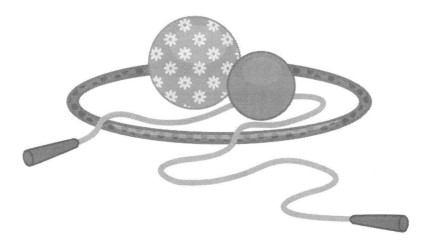

Activity #1

Thinking
THE PURPOSE CIRCLE

DESCRIPTION: Often children exhibit behavior that gets them into hot water with little awareness regarding what led up to the behavior and "how they got here." Children have a need or an impulse and they act on that impulse, sometimes in a split second. You can help them raise their "mindful awareness" by teaching them that we need to behave "on purpose." We need to behave with intention. "The Purpose Circle" helps children recognize that they make a choice when they behave. Adding intention to the choice helps empower them to choose behaviors that serve them well, not behaviors that get them into trouble.

RELATED SKILL SETS YOU MAY WISH TO EXPLORE WITH THE CHILDREN:

- Cognitive Flexibility
- Decision-Making
- Emotional Regulation
- Focused Attention
- Impulse Control
- Inhibition

- Organization
- Planning
- Previewing
- Prioritizing
- Problem-Solving
- Sustained Attention

MATERIALS: A hula hoop.

READY: Ask the child to place the hula-hoop on the floor. "Every time you do something, you have a choice to think it out or to behave in a hurry without thinking. When you think things out and make a decision to act, rather than doing so in a hurry, you make better choices. Let's practice making thoughtful choices by stepping into the Purpose Circle each time you choose to do something. Ready? Let's Play."

LET'S PLAY: "For the next few minutes, every time you make a choice to do something new, you will climb into the Purpose Circle and state your intention. It sounds like this: 'I am going to go to the art table and draw a picture of a lion.'"

"You go to the art table and draw as you wish, then when your mind thinks of something else you want to do, instead of just doing it, you will come back to the Purpose Circle and say out loud the next thing you plan to do."

"It sounds like this, 'I drew a lion now I am going to go put it in my backpack so I can give it to my sister.'"

Play the Purpose Circle for a few minutes until the child has practiced acting "with intention." The Purpose Circle is a fabulous way to teach children that what they choose to do, they do on purpose. Adding thought to their actions reduces impulsivity and brings front of mind what actions they are choosing.

Think about it for a second. Many of the children with whom you interact may tell you "I don't know" or "I don't remember" when you explore the actions that might have brought them to your office or playroom. By playing the Purpose Circle, children begin to experience moving, doing, choosing and behaving "with intention." Few children would walk into the Purpose Circle and say, "Now I am going to hit Joey in the face." Imagine if they had to do that; their behaviors would change, eh?

REVIEW:

1. What did it feel like to step into the Purpose Circle and state your intention?

2. Before today, did you know what it meant to "Make a choice?"

3. Before today, did you know that every time you do something, you make a choice to do it?

4. Was it hard, silly or even funny to have to step into the Purpose Circle every time you chose a new action?

5. What were you feeling when you had to step into the Purpose Circle over and over again?

6. What did you learn?

7. Can you imagine your brother, sister or friend needing to do this?

8. What would that look like?

9. Who do you know who would love the Purpose Circle?

10. What would they love about it?

11. Do you know anyone who needs to think more before they act?

12. Would that person like or dislike the Purpose Circle?

13. If you were teaching how to use the Purpose Circle to your classmates, what would you say or do?

14. How would you improve the Purpose Circle, if you were teaching it?

15. Do you think the Purpose Circle can help you choose your actions more carefully?

16. How? Why?

Activity #2

Thinking
COPY CAT!

DESCRIPTION: Copy Cat is a fun way for children to use their fine motor skills, powers of observation and memory to copy a design that they see or have seen and must try to remember.

RELATED SKILL SETS YOU MAY WISH TO EXPLORE WITH THE CHILDREN:

- Initiation
- Memory Strategy
- Organization
- Sequencing
- Sustained Attention

MATERIALS: Building material of choice or a picture of the figure you would like the child to reproduce.

READY: Using Play-Doh, blocks, or Legos, build a figure and have the child build an exact replica in size and color. For younger kids, show them the model and keep it out so they can see it. For older kids, try increasing the difficulty of the task by keeping the model out for 60 seconds and then putting it out of sight while the child tries to reproduce it from memory.

LET'S PLAY: "Let's see if you can copy this figure using this material. Spend a moment looking at it and decide what you will need to build it yourself. Try to think out loud while you are making it, like this 'First I will, then I will….' Go ahead!"

REVIEW: Explore the child's experience with simple questions such as:

1. What did you enjoy about this activity?

2. What strategies did you use to remember the object?

3. Was it easy or hard to remember the object by imagining it?

4. What steps did you take to replicate the object?

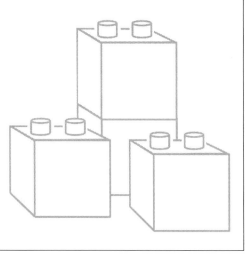

Activity #3

Thinking
ORDER IT!

DESCRIPTION: Order It is an imaginative way for children to organize, prioritize and remember items that they might like. Children will have to use their thinking caps to either follow the order rule (such as, order these from smallest to largest) or create their own rules in order to have a logical sequence for the items they list.

RELATED SKILL SETS YOU MAY WISH TO EXPLORE WITH THE CHILDREN:

- Memory Strategy
- Organization
- Sequencing
- Sustained Attention

MATERIALS: Magazines or catalogs, scissors, glue stick, paper, pencil, poster board.

READY: Have the child look through a toy catalogue or magazine and cut out or make a list of all the things he/she would like to have or play with. Next, ask the child to put the items in some kind of order. For younger children, you may suggest an order such as, "The thing you want most, to the least," or "Alphabetical," or "By price." For older kids, you could also have them write a description of the item, cut the pictures out, and create a list with descriptions and pasted pictures, or even plan a presentation. A variation for the older kids would be for them to look at the pictures they have cut out for 60 seconds, put the pictures away and then have them recreate the list from memory.

LET'S PLAY: "We are going to play a thinking game. This game starts with you writing a wish list of things you would like to order from these cool catalogs and magazines. The rules are that you can choose any items you would like, but you have to think of a way to organize your list that makes sense. For example, my list would include things that are my favorite color, blue. Or I will organize my list of blue things from smallest to largest. Either way is a good category for the items. As long as you say what the rule is, and I could use or understand the rule, you can order anything you like for your wish list. When we are done, each of you will try to guess the other's rule."

REVIEW: Explore the child's experience with simple questions such as:

1. Whose rule was easiest to guess?
2. What made it easy?
3. Whose rule was most difficult to guess and why?
4. Whose wish list did you like?
5. How hard was it to find things that fit your rule?
6. Did it get easier after you found the first few?
7. Did you choose objects first and then make a rule, or did you make a rule and then choose your items?

Thinking
COLOR WORD GAME

DESCRIPTION: The Color Word Game can be played with one child in a group or with an entire class. It is a fun activity to enhance visual skills, short-term memory and production output.

RELATED SKILL SETS YOU MAY WISH TO EXPLORE WITH THE CHILDREN:

- Alerting Attention
- Applying Past Knowledge
- Cognitive Flexibility
- Cognitive Persistence
- Decision-Making
- Exploration

- Focused Attention
- Impulse Control
- Inhibition
- Memory Strategy
- Visual Scanning
- Working Memory

MATERIALS: Index cards, colored markers.

READY: Write color words on cards using colors different than the word that is written. For example, write the word "RED" with blue marker. Create as many of these as possible suitable for the color knowledge of the child or children.

LET'S PLAY: Show the child the card quickly by flipping it over. At first ask the child to say what is written on the card as quickly as they can and flip over 5–10 cards. Score 1 point for each time the child correctly reads the word on the card. Next, shuffle the cards. Now ask the child to say the color of the ink on the card. Flip over 5–10 cards and give 1 point for each time the child correctly says the name of the color ink. Lastly, ask the child to alternate between saying the word that is written and the color of the ink. Give 1 point for each correct response. To make it more fun, the number of points can add up to small prizes like candy, a homemade stress ball or take a break card.

REVIEW:

1. Which was more difficult, saying the color name or ink?

2. Did you use any strategies that made this game easier?

3. Create a list of strategies for thinking or pausing before you speak or answer.

Activity #5

Thinking

MY ANGER MANAGER

DESCRIPTION: Children experience a broad range of feelings, some of which may feel too BIG to handle. We know from cognitive science that becoming aware of one's feeling state empowers a person to better manage and modulate their feelings. With My Anger Manager, we help the child step back and look at what makes them feel anger, how they respond to anger and what other things they can say, think and do in order to use their anger productively while not letting it overcome them or interfere with their relationships. The printable form on page 65 is a handy resource for feelings exploration, conversation and problem-solving with children or teens.

RELATED SKILL SETS YOU MAY WISH TO EXPLORE WITH THE CHILDREN:

- Critical Thinking
- Decision-Making
- Emotional Regulation
- Exploration
- Impulse Control
- Narrative Language
- Problem-Solving
- Reflection

MATERIALS: Markers, pens, printable sheet.

READY: Introduce the concept that we can talk about, write about and draw about how we feel in order to cope better with our feelings. Print out the My Anger Manager image to explore what led up to the child's feelings and what the child can shift in order to manage his or her feelings better.

LET'S PLAY: "Experiences create all sorts of different feelings within us. With My Anger Manager, we can explore what happened and how it made us feel. Let's go block by block and write down and talk about:

- What happened?
- What did the person say?
- How did it make you feel?
- What made you angry?
- What were you thinking?
- What did you say?
- How did your body feel?

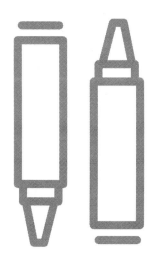

REVIEW:

1. How can you think differently to feel calmer?

2. What else can you think?

3. If you think calmer thoughts, how will your body feel?

4. What can you say to yourself to feel calmer?

5. What can you say to the other person to get what you need?

6. What can you say to the other person to help them remain calm?

7. How can this experience look differently next time?

8. What is your plan for staying calm?

9. Let's rewrite the ending to this story, how can it have a happier ending?

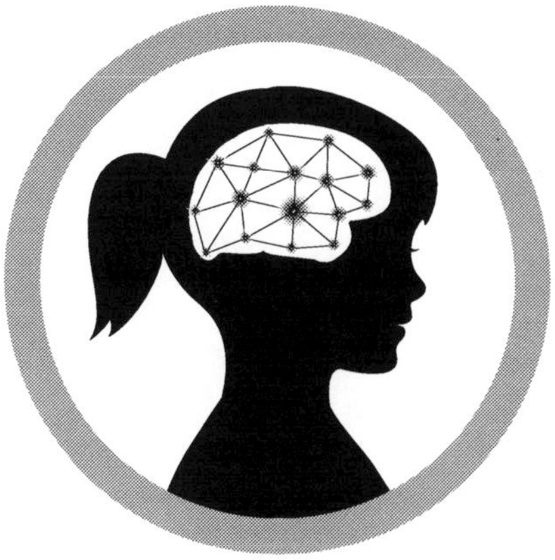

MY ANGER

When I Think It Out I Will Do Better

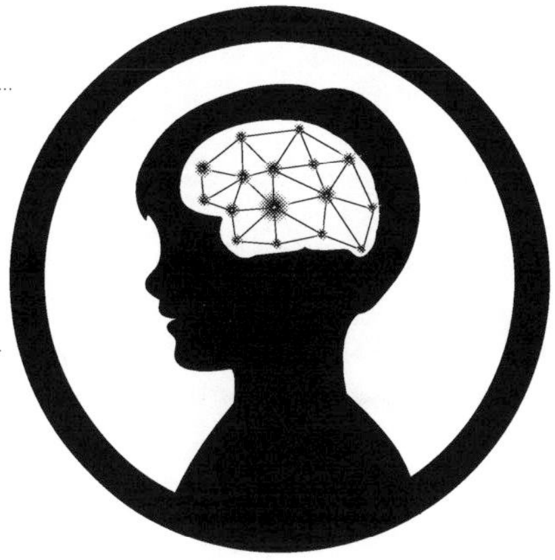

This is what happened:

_____

He/she said this:

_____

He/she did this:

_____

What made me angry was:

_____

This is what I thought:

_____

This is what I said:

_____

This is how my body felt:

_____

This is what I did:

_____

THIS IS WHAT I CAN DO NEXT TIME

Think this:

_____

Say this:

_____

Do this:

_____

Thinking
I'M GOING ON A PICNIC

DESCRIPTION: We are all familiar with the game "I'm going on a picnic and I am going to bring. . ." Each child says one thing they are going to bring plus everything that others have said before them. The student who goes first usually starts by thinking of something to bring with the letter A, the next student repeats the A item and contributes an item starting with the letter B, and so on. In our spin on "I'm going on a picnic" you can have fun as a group making your own cards to hand out. On each card is an activity that requires one to understand that some activities are done in a specific sequence. As an example, one card might be a photo of a bed that is made. The children would then need to work together to write down, act out, or say aloud the steps to making ones' bed. Choose simple tasks here. You are teaching sequencing, there are steps or sequences to almost every action we take. We have the children elaborate on the sequence of steps needed to execute the task. Rather than structuring the contributions according to the alphabet, in our version the contributions are organized by the ordered sequences in the task.

EXAMPLE: I'm going to bake a cupcake; I'm going to make my bed; I'm going to pack my backpack; I'm going to make my sister breakfast. . . .

Here is a list of possible activity pictures for your cards. You can simply cut out photos from magazines or you may hand draw them. Sometimes the children even like to come up with the tasks and draw them. This is all brain development, so enjoy the artistic process.

- Bake cupcakes
- Clear the dishes from breakfast table
- Complete one math assignment
- Do one load of laundry
- Empty the dishwasher
- Feed the cat
- Help a family member plant flowers
- Make one's bed
- Make pancakes for two people
- Pack one's backpack for the next day of school
- Paint a picture
- Read a story book to a younger sibling
- Take the dog for a walk
- Write a poem

Each student must repeat the initial phrase, "I'm going to... and add the sequenced steps to the task stated by the previous students, in proper order. To help their encoding abilities, we provide markers and paper and the children are allowed to draw pictures or write ONE word to help them remember the sequence of steps.

This is a cool activity that encourages cognitive flexibility along with logical, sequential thinking. The flexibility comes into play when participants have different ways of completing tasks and the logic is needed so as not to leave out important steps.

Activity #7

Thinking
THE PARTS OF A TASK GAME

DESCRIPTION: This activity is a bit like "I'm going on a picnic" in reverse; however, in this game, the children actually become parts of the tasks.

RELATED SKILL SETS YOU MAY WISH TO EXPLORE WITH THE CHILDREN:

- Alerting Attention
- Applying Past Knowledge
- Cognitive Flexibility
- Cognitive Persistence
- Emotional Regulation
- Focused Attention
- Inhibition

- Memory Strategy
- Organization
- Planning
- Prioritizing
- Sequencing
- Sustained Attention
- Working Memory

READY: Each child draws a card. Some cards have a part of a task that belongs in the sequence to complete an objective and one child will have the completed task card. Once each child has drawn a card, the objective is for the students to work together to line up in the correct order of tasks from start to finish. Students have to talk with each other and line up in order based upon where in the sequence their action card would fall. Children must talk to each other and problem-solve to decide if they must line up before or behind others.

LET'S PLAY: "Today we are going to play a game that gets you thinking and moving! Each of you will pick a card which will have on it a step in a process of completing an activity. One of you will have the completed task card. Your jobs will be to stand up, talk to each other and figure out where to stand in relation to your friends. When you are done forming a line, you should be lined up in the correct order, from start to finish, of your task."

EXAMPLE: Completed Task or Activity Card: "Make a turkey and cheese sandwich."
Action Cards (a part of the task or activity):

- Get the ingredients
- Get a plate
- Place two slices of bread on a plate
- Put three slices of turkey on a slice of bread
- Put one slice of cheese on a slice of bread
- Put bread, cheese and turkey together

- Cut the sandwich in half

- Put away the ingredients

- Wash the plate and knife

"Mine says…" "I must be at the end." "Mine says clean up, I think that would be last." "Cheese and turkey have no logical order, I think we can stand side-by-side!"

As with many of these activities, we encourage the facilitator to use his or her own imagination and creativity to inspire the game and the goals he/she would like to work on. It's super fun to watch the game evolve as the children contribute their ideas as well.

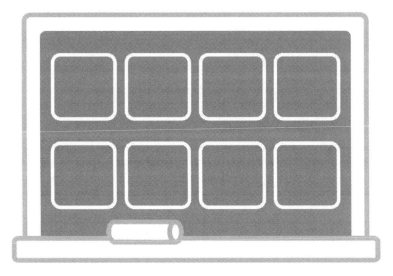

Activity #8

Thinking
WHAT'S THE BEST THING TO SAY (TO STAY CALM AND CONNECTED)

DESCRIPTION: Every day, there are moments when we talk with one another in which the words and tone we use impact how the other person responds. Helping children (teachers and parents) become mindful of their nonverbal gestures, words and tone helps them to be more effective communicators.

RELATED SKILL SETS YOU MAY WISH TO EXPLORE WITH THE CHILDREN:

- Applying Past Knowledge
- Cognitive Flexibility
- Creative Thinking
- Critical Thinking
- Decision-Making

- Emotional Regulation
- Exploration
- Inhibition
- Narrative Language
- Reflection

READY: Have the child or children sit at a table or in a circle facing one another. Tell them, "We are going to play 'What's the best thing to say' now. For this game, I have made a deck of cards with different scenarios on them. We will each be taking turns reading from the deck of cards. One person will read the sentence out loud and the other person will respond with a sentence that focuses on responding in a way that keeps everyone calm and connected instead of angry, afraid or defensive. Because there are no perfect answers, we will kindly talk about the response and explore how it was a helpful response. If we feel there is another way to say it, we can offer those ideas as well." Model reading from a card and answering it in a kind manner, then let the children go around picking from the deck and answering the question. This can be done one-on-one or in a dyad, group or class. Model non-defensive responding and kindness, not criticism.

4-Part STAY CALM & CONNECTED PLAN

You can even teach the child or children our 4-PART STAY CALM & CONNECTED PLAN:

- MY FEELING
- HOW I PERCEIVED THE SITUATION
- MY INTENTION
- MY GOAL or PLAN

Helping everyone include sentences reflecting the 4-Part Plan shifts how parents, teachers and children communicate with one another.

Here is an example: How would you respond?

Here's the scene: You are at home watching TV. Your mom just walked in the door.

Here's the sentence: She says, "Hi honey, did you feed the dog like I asked you?"

Calm (yet honest) and Connected Answer: "Mom, I feel annoyed (FEELING) when you immediately remind me of my chore when you see me (PERCEPTION). I'm sitting here watching TV to relax (INTENTION) and when you do that I get stressed out. I know I should remember to feed the dog (INTENTION), but can we agree on a nicer way to remind me (GOAL)?"

Mom's Response: "Hi Honey. I see that you are enjoying this show (ADULT NON-JUDGMENTAL PERCEPTION). I worry (FEELING) that the dog won't get fed and I think it's important for you to contribute to the household chores (INTENTION). Could we agree that when you feed the dog (PLAN & GOAL), you put a check on the calendar here so we all know that the dog is being treated respectfully? Thank you."

We have written five questions, you can make up your own and write them on index cards or cardstock for the children to use as conversation cards.

LET'S PLAY:

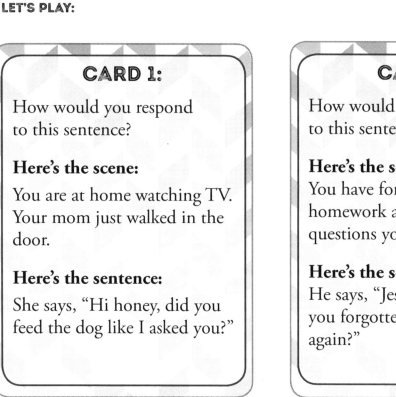

CARD 1:

How would you respond to this sentence?

Here's the scene:
You are at home watching TV. Your mom just walked in the door.

Here's the sentence:
She says, "Hi honey, did you feed the dog like I asked you?"

CARD 2:

How would you respond to this sentence?

Here's the scene:
You have forgotten your homework and your teacher questions you about it.

Here's the sentence:
He says, "Jessica, why have you forgotten your homework again?"

CARD 3:

How would you respond to this sentence?

Here's the scene:
You have been wanting to play XBOX all morning, but your brother won't get off it. You ask him if you can take a turn.

Here's the sentence:
He says, "You played XBOX all day yesterday; today it's my day."

CARD 4:

How would you respond to this sentence?

Here's the scene:
You are excited to go to the beach with your friends. Your dad comes in as you are getting ready and tells you it's time to rake the leaves.

Here's the sentence:
He says, "Jeremiah, I'm glad you are still here, you can rake the leaves while I mow the lawn."

CARD 5:

How would you respond to this sentence?

Here's the scene:
You are taking a road trip with your family. They all ate breakfast when you were not hungry yet. Now you have been in the car for two hours and you are ready to eat. You ask your **grandmother to stop at a restaurant.**

Here's the sentence:
She says, "Michaela, you had a chance to eat two hours ago and you chose not to;, we will eat when we get to the hotel."

REVIEW: Talk about the difference between a "knee-jerk" response and a "calm & connected" response. A "knee-jerk" response is often impulsive and might be critical, angry or sarcastic; this kind of response of often defensive and can make matters worse. A "calm and connected" response is still honest and might entail strong feelings, but it has a reasonable request that shifts the dialogue from defensive to cooperative. You can even practice types of responses with your clients or students showing them the differences between aggressive, defensive and cooperative responses.

Take your time talking about how we use our nonverbal gestures, facial expressions, words and tone to respond to others. Discuss how to respond to others when what they say is not what we are hoping for. Talk about how we have different needs and how best to respond, even when we might have strong feelings. This is a valuable role play and exploration activity to help children (and grown-ups) become empowered to respond prosocially to difficult situations.

Activity #9

Thinking

WHAT'S WORKING FOR ME?

DESCRIPTION: Children often have feelings and thoughts of which they are not mindfully aware. Those thoughts and feelings about life experiences or specific situations can cause feelings of unease that increase anxiety.

At the heart of it, the cognitive side of anxiety (because there can be quite a strong biological side as well) is about the perception that one does not possess the necessary skills to cope with or manage specific task demands in daily life. As an example, a child might be anxious about a vocabulary test if the words are difficult for the child to read, remember and retrieve. A child might be anxious about going to lunch when he feels he might not have the skills to seek out a table mate and feel less alone while eating lunch.

What's Working For Me helps children think about what might be working and what might not be working about a specific life circumstance. The children are then empowered to find new thoughts, words and actions to cope in a new way with the situation. You can use it for a variety of circumstances; let your creativity guide the way.

Let's look at the lunch example. We would say this, quietly, one-on-one with the child.
"Joey, I see that you are hesitant to go to lunch each day. I'd like to know more about what that is like for you. Are you open to playing a thinking game with me about lunchtime?"

"Let's write down a few things that are working for you when you go to lunch. Then we can fill out our What's Working for Me planning sheet and develop a plan to make lunchtime better for you."

JOEY – LUNCH EXAMPLE

T: "Let's think about what you like about lunch."

J: "Well, I'm usually hungry, so it's good to eat."

J: "I like the days when they serve grilled cheese."

J: "When Sam is at school, I usually sit with him."

T: "Great! Let's write that in the green box, what's working for me."

T: "Now, what don't you like about lunchtime?"

J: "I hate sitting alone."

J: "Sam is sick a lot, so then I have to sit alone."

J: "No one asks me to sit with them."

J: "It's embarrassing."

T: "Thanks for sharing that with me, I can see how it could feel sad to eat lunch alone."

T: "We have a third box on our What's Working For Me planning sheet. Let's brainstorm how lunch could look differently so you can feel better about going to lunch."

T: "If lunch were better for you, what would that look like?"

J: "Well, I'd have a friend to sit with all the time."

T: "Who else besides Sam might you like to sit with?"

J: "Jessica, but she sits with her friends."

T: What if you asked Jessica, "Hey Jessica, when Sam's not here, may I sit with you guys at lunch?"

J: "She'd probably say, 'No.'"

T: "What might be a good time to ask her? Would the best time be right before lunch, or might you ask her in class one day to plan ahead for the situation?"

J: "I could try to ask her in the morning before school."

T: "Okay, let's write that down and maybe even practice the words you will use."

T: "Then we can even write a few more ideas about other things you can do to make lunchtime a happier time for you."

As teachers, clinicians and parents, you know that conversations with children might be really straightforward or you might need to help them along in the conversation. Be patient, ask reflective questions or ask the child to tell you a bit more: "Help me understand that better."

Just letting children know that they can solve a difficult situation by looking at what is working and what they'd like to see be different is empowering and can lead to better daily experiences.

What's Working For Me

What's Not Working For Me

My Plan To Make This Feel Better

Activity #10

Thinking
WHAT'S IN THE BAG?

DESCRIPTION: What's in the bag is a narrative language game based on hide and seek. The object of the activity is to use words to describe a known object without seeing it.

RELATED SKILL SETS YOU MAY WISH TO EXPLORE WITH THE CHILDREN:

- Alerting Attention
- Applying Past Knowledge
- Cognitive Persistence
- Critical Thinking
- Emotional Regulation
- Focused Attention
- Inhibition
- Problem-Solving
- Working Memory

MATERIALS: One lunch-size brown paper bag; five small toys or items to place in the bag, one at a time.

READY: Ask the child to gather five small items or toys that are fun or meaningful to him. Place the items on a flat surface within arm's reach behind you. Sit facing the child approximately three feet apart.

LET'S PLAY: One at a time, place an object in the paper bag and close it up. Hand the bag to the child and ask him to describe what is in the bag without naming the item. For example, if the item is a small toy soldier, the child might say, "This is a hard toy, it has sharp edges, and it is small enough to fit in my hand. I think it is for playing army-men." Tell the child he may open the bag and see "What's in the bag?"

Alternatively, the adult can gather five meaningful items unknown to the child; this can be done after the child is familiar with the game or when the child might enjoy the "ah-ha" experience of discovery. "Oh! It's a toy soldier!"

REVIEW:

1. How did you know what it was?

2. What made it easy or difficult to describe this toy?

3. Do you see this toy any differently now that you touched it without your eyes?

4. What else could it have been?

If the child does not describe the object clearly or is not sure what it is, help him with prompts.

1. What does it feel like?

2. Is it hard or soft?

3. Is it sharp or rounded?

4. Is it squishy?

5. Can you guess how many inches long it is?

6. Is it too big to fit in the palm of your hand?

7. What do you think people do with this toy?

When you are finished exploring the first item move on to the second. Play until the child's attention or interest starts to wane. Then move onto another activity or game.

Thinking
I-SPY DETECTIVE

DESCRIPTION: I-Spy Detective is an engaging memory game in which children are asked to look at and remember random objects. Children can be taught strategies to remember, like using a mnemonic for a list, associating objects with a story and putting objects in certain orders in their minds.

RELATED SKILL SETS YOU MAY WISH TO EXPLORE WITH THE CHILDREN:

- Alerting Attention
- Applying Past Knowledge
- Critical Thinking
- Decision-Making
- Emotional Regulation
- Exploration
- Focused Attention
- Impulse Control
- Memory Strategy

- Organization
- Planning
- Problem-Solving
- Reflection
- Sequencing
- Successive Processing
- Sustained Attention
- Visual Scanning
- Working Memory

MATERIALS: A tray or plate and 10–25 different small objects.

READY: Collect a tray full of objects of various shapes and sizes. Lay the objects on the tray. Begin with a few objects and slowly increase the number of objects on the tray.

LET'S PLAY: Show the child the tray and ask them to look closely at everything on it for 15–30 seconds (depending on the child's age). Next, take the tray away and ask the child to write down as many objects as they can remember. Give points or stickers for each correct answer. In a group, the student who has the most correct objects is the winner of the round. Next, show the child the tray again and take away a number of objects. Take the tray away and ask the child to try to remember which object was taken away. Create various memory challenges by taking away other or adding new objects.

REVIEW: When the game is over, ask the child what strategies (s)he used to try to remember. Help the child organize the objects according to a strategy so that it will be easier to remember all the objects. Replay the memory challenges and demonstrate how memory strategies like familiarity, categorizing or grouping can assist memory.

Thinking

I LOVE MY PLANNER CHEAT SHEET

Activity #12

DESCRIPTION: Planning and organization can be a big challenge for many students. Using a planner is a simple way for kids to stay organized, be mindful of what is ahead, and be advocates for themselves and their weekly work schedules. Print this out or develop one that is tailored to the child's specific needs and activities. Managing one's daily tasks in a visual manner is a helpful way to get and stay organized.

Mark the things you put in your planner each day:	Monday	Tuesday	Wednesday	Thursday	Friday	Saturday	Sunday
Homework Assignments							
Final Due Date/ Break Down Due Dates							
Test and Quiz Dates							
Extracurricular Activities							
Study Groups and Review Sessions							
Extra Help with Teachers							
Meetings							
To-Do Checklist							

Thinking

I USE MY PLANNER CHEAT SHEET

DESCRIPTION: This printable is a handy tool to help children keep their daily tasks and activities "front of mind." The children can fill in their "plan" for tackling different tasks and keep a copy in their locker, backpack or work-station at home. Print this out or make one for each child depending on their needs and activities.

Activity #13

	Monday	Tuesday	Wednesday	Thursday	Friday	Saturday	Sunday
Keep a copy taped inside your locker, desk and at home. Check your planner at regular times. In each box write down one action you will do to stay on track.:							
Before school in the morning I will:							
At the beginning and end of class, write down my assignments							
After school at home I will:							
When I finish an assignment, I will check it off in my planner							
Before I go to bed, I will pack up my materials for tomorrow							
Other tasks I wish to remember include:							

Thinking
BOSS BACK THE INNER BULLY: METACOGNITION

DESCRIPTION: Children can often feel at the mercy of difficult emotions when they show up. Teaching students that feelings are not facts and that they have some power to boss back the unhelpful thoughts that are keeping the negative feeling strong empowers children to use positive coping strategies and feel better. It is difficult at first for some children to understand the difference between the feeling and the thought. One clue we have is that a feeling can be summed up in one word, but a thought is a sentence that we are saying to ourselves in our heads. By bossing back unhelpful thoughts and choosing to say something else that might be a little more helpful and also true, we can feel better and then decide what to do next.

EXAMPLE:

When ***I don't do as well as I would like on my spelling test*** I feel SAD.

Sometimes when I feel sad, I notice that the words in my head are
"***I'm so stupid. I am never going to learn how to spell.***"

I notice that this is not a nice thing to say to myself or about myself. I would not say that to a friend. I boss back that inner bully by saying

"***It's okay to make mistakes. I will keep trying to learn my spelling words.***"
to myself instead.

BOSS BACK WORKSHEET

When I _____ I feel SAD.

Sometimes when I feel sad, I notice that the words in my head are

"_____." I notice that this is not a nice thing to say to

myself or about myself. I would not say that to a friend. I boss back that inner bully by

saying "_____" to myself instead.

When I _____ I feel MAD.

Sometimes when I feel mad, I notice that the words in my head are

"_____." I notice that this is not a nice thing to say to

myself or about myself. I would not say that to a friend. I boss back that inner bully by

saying "_____" to myself instead.

When I _____ I feel

FRUSTRATED. Sometimes when I feel frustrated, I notice that the words in my head

are "_____." I notice that this is not a nice thing to say to

myself or about myself. I would not say that to a friend. I boss back that inner bully by

saying "_____" to myself instead.

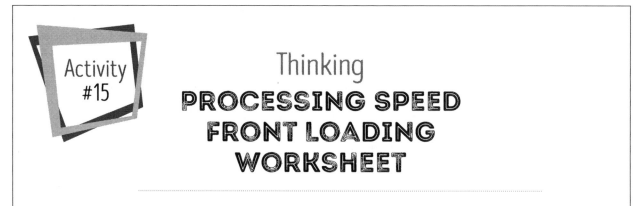

Thinking
PROCESSING SPEED FRONT LOADING WORKSHEET

DESCRIPTION: Front Loading is an executive functioning strategy that helps students organize their thinking by considering tangible and concrete goals. When one is goal-oriented and forward-thinking, it is a easier to stay on task and focus on what to listen for or learn. Like the index section of a book, the front-loading worksheet will give the student an understanding of main ideas to look for and can help keep the student working in a goal-directed manner during a lesson.

Use this worksheet to plan, preview and organize a strategy for listening and learning in class.

During this class, three important ideas that I will listen for are:

1.

2.

3.

When the teacher begins talking about _____, I will write down three notes:

1.

2.

3.

When the teacher begins talking about _____, I will write down three questions:

1.

2.

3.

Use this concept to write your own "Let me plan how to do this" methodologies with the children or students.

Thinking
GAME DAY

JOHNNY'S STORY: Johnny was meeting with his school psychologist for his weekly appointment. Johnny liked going to see her, but sometimes they talked about things that he felt sad about – like times when he had a bad day at school, overreacted to something or got in trouble. Johnny didn't always think it was easy to talk about those times because when he was feeling happy, he knew that he had made a mistake and he knew what he should have done instead. Johnny's school psychologist, Mrs. Comizio, said: "Johnny, you know how we meet and make drawings about the sizes of feelings and the sizes of reactions? And how we talk about tools you can put in your tool box for when you have a big feeling?"

Johnny: "Yes, I like decorating my tool box and putting my tools on little cards inside. My favorite tool is the card that reminds me to take volcano breaths!"

Mrs. Comizio: "I like that one too! And you have been doing a wonderful job learning some tools and practicing them with me. When we practice in my office, you learn a lot. Just like when you practice for your soccer games, you learn new skills from your coach. Soccer practice is fun and you don't always have the same feelings during practice as you do in the games. What kinds of feelings do you have during practice and then during a soccer game?"

Johnny: "Well, I love practice! I feel excited and happy during practice because I am with my friends and sometimes we get a treat from the coaches or parents after practice. I feel happy and excited and then tired if I run around a lot. During the games, I also feel this way, but usually I am a little nervous because I really want to do my best and win the game! Sometimes, when I don't score, I get mad at myself too." Johnny frowns.

Mrs. Comizio: "That makes sense to me. Sometimes we can all be really hard on ourselves when we feel like we didn't do our best. I also know that your coach understands that sometimes you win and sometimes you lose. If you always won every single time and always played perfectly, then you wouldn't even need to practice! But that isn't what human beings are like and also isn't the point of the game. Human beings learn by practice, and making mistakes or losing is an important part of the learning process. I am kind of like a coach too – a feelings coach! You and I practice your tools together and because my office isn't the game field, it's the practice field, I bet you feel differently about using the tools here than you do on the game field. Can you guess where your game field is for feelings? I mean, where you would actually use your tools in a real game?"

Johnny: "You mean my classroom?"

Mrs. Comizio: "Exactly! In your classroom, you are learning all your subjects and working with others and that is when you are more likely to have more difficult feelings than you do in here while we practice. That is the game field where you must use your tools. And even though it can be hard to talk about mistakes, times in class when you shoot and miss, those are really important learning opportunities that you and I should talk about in practice."

GAME DAY WORKSHEET

Tell about a time in class when you had an impulse to do something you knew you shouldn't.

_____

_____

_____

Write about whether you were able to use a tool (shoot and score!) or if the feeling took over and took control:

_____

_____

_____

Write about a way you could use a strategy on the game field so that if that happens again, you have a chance to shoot and score!

_____

_____

_____

Thinking
THE HOPPER

DESCRIPTION: When you are working with children regarding their previewing, planning, organizing and sequencing skills, it is helpful to categorize or label their activities. We often talk with children about needing to get their homework "in the hopper" at school, meaning they need to put their finished homework in the "in" basket on their teacher's desk. So we made a little activity we called the HOPPER Homework Planning and Review Sheet. Kids think it's catchy, so they are willing to play along. Sometimes we even add some basketball metaphors in the discussion. You can feel free to vary the metaphors as well as the sheet for your clients' or students' individual needs.

THE HOPPER – Homework Planning and Review Sheet

RELATED SKILL SETS YOU MAY WISH TO EXPLORE WITH THE CHILDREN:

- Applying Past Knowledge
- Cognitive Flexibility
- Critical Thinking
- Decision-Making
- Organization
- Planning
- Previewing
- Prioritizing
- Problem-Solving
- Project Planning
- Reflection
- Task Management
- Time Allocation
- Time Estimation
- Time Monitoring

MATERIALS: THE HOPPER Sheet, pen or pencil.

The facilitator reviews the sheet with the student(s). Tell the students that they are going to put their homework in the HOPPER!

– THE HOPPER –
Homework Planning and Review Sheet

HOMEWORK COMPLETION GOALS

To complete homework by:

Date: _____

P L A N **S U B J E C T**

Assignment: _____ Materials Needed: _____

_____ _____

_____ _____

_____ _____

_____ _____

_____ _____

_____ _____

Assignment: _____ Materials Needed: _____

_____ _____

_____ _____

_____ _____

_____ _____

_____ _____

_____ _____

P L A N | **S U B J E C T**

Assignment: _____   Materials Needed: _____

_____   _____

_____   _____

_____   _____

_____   _____

_____   _____

_____   _____

Assignment: _____   Materials Needed: _____

_____   _____

_____   _____

_____   _____

_____   _____

_____   _____

_____   _____

Assignment: _____   Materials Needed: _____

_____   _____

_____   _____

_____   _____

_____   _____

_____   _____

How I did (my rating): _____

Self-Rating 1-10: _____

Parent Rating 1-10: _____

Teacher Rating 1-10: _____

• •

What helped, what worked?

_____

_____

_____

What made it hard? What did I try when it was difficult?

_____

_____

_____

What went wrong or was missing?

_____

_____

Future suggestions for overcoming obstacles to goal:

_____

_____

Next time if I have this challenge/problem, which was: _____

I will plan to:

_____

_____

_____

Why is it helpful to do your homework?

_____

When you are able to complete your homework, what is helpful to you?

_____

Are there tools, people or reminders that help you get your homework done?

_____

What makes it difficult to get homework done?

_____

Are there certain types of homework that are more difficult than others?

_____

What about where you do your homework, is that working for you?

_____

How about when you do your homework? Are you rested and calm or rushed?

_____

What has the Hopper showed you? Did you learn anything by using it?

_____

What would you like to do differently to get a better outcome?

_____

What's your plan for tomorrow? Let's try small changes one at a time and evaluate how they work for you.

_____

_____

_____

Activity #18

Thinking
LET ME THINK ABOUT THAT

DESCRIPTION: It's helpful for children to have a strategy to think about an activity or action before they do it. Building "time to reflect" as well as "intent to act" into the thinking process is empowering. This worksheet provides an opportunity for the child to explore the parts of a task, the plan of action to complete the task and the steps to revise their approach in the future.

RELATED SKILL SETS YOU MAY WISH TO EXPLORE WITH THE CHILDREN:

- Cognitive Flexibility
- Organization
- Planning
- Previewing
- Prioritizing
- Problem-Solving
- Project Planning

- Reflection
- Sequencing
- Successive Processing
- Task Management
- Time Allocation
- Time Estimation
- Time Monitoring

LET ME THINK ABOUT THAT WORKSHEET

Taking time to think and reflect before you respond, decide or take action.

What have I been asked to do? _____

By whom? _____

What is the time frame? _____

Is there a due date? _____

Will I do this alone or with others? _____

What Will It Take?

The Task: _____

Parts of the task	Time allocation for each task
1. _____	1. _____
2. _____	2. _____
3. _____	3. _____
4. _____	4. _____
5. _____	5. _____

What materials will I need?

1. _____

2. _____

3. _____

4. _____

5. _____

Exactly when would I make time for each part of the task?

1. _____

2. _____

3. _____

4. _____

5. _____

How beneficial is this task to me?

Very Beneficial   Not So Beneficial

How beneficial is this task to someone else or others?   Very Beneficial   Not So Beneficial

What is my decision? _____

Why? _____

What will my verbal response be? _____

How will I deliver it?   In Person   Via Text   Via Phone   Via Email   Other

Activity #19

Thinking

WHAT'S IN IT FOR ME?

DESCRIPTION: Enhancing cognitive flexibility often entails helping the child see the benefits in an alternate task or activity. Seeing "What's in it for me" helps the student or client to not only exhibit cognitive flexibility, but also increase motivation. This worksheet aids in the exploration of the costs and benefits of a given task with an eye toward helping the child learn to shift task sets, and think flexibly about changing activities.

RELATED SKILL SETS YOU MAY WISH TO EXPLORE WITH THE CHILDREN:

- Cognitive Flexibility

- Inhibition

- Organization

- Planning

- Previewing

- Prioritizing

- Problem-Solving

- Project Planning

- Reflection

- Sequencing

- Successive Processing

- Task Management

- Time Allocation

WHAT'S IN IT FOR ME? WORKSHEET

Finding the value in switching tasks

What am I doing now?

The activity: _____

Examples:

Playing on the playground   Reading a book

Playing on the computer   Doing my homework

How much do I like what I am doing now?   Don't like it   Love it!

How fun is what I am doing right now?   Boring   Super Fun

What have I been asked to do? _____

By whom? _____

When do I need to do it? _____

What will make it easier to shift tasks? _____

What will make it hard to switch tasks? _____

What's in it for me when I switch tasks?

1. _____

2. _____

3. _____

What can I say to myself to make switching tasks easier?

1. _____

2. _____

3. _____

What will happen if I resist switching tasks?

1. _____

2. _____

3. _____

When will I be able to go back to doing what I like?

1. _____

2. _____

3. _____

After I _____ I'll be able to _____ until _____.

What's my "make this easier on myself" plan of action?

_____

_____

_____

_____

_____

_____

_____

_____

_____

_____

_____

Activity
#20

Thinking
WHAT'S UNDERNEATH

DESCRIPTION: Scaffolding tasks requires understanding the expected behavior, the tasks it takes to execute that behavior and the sub-tasks underneath that behavior. Examining the sub-tasks often helps us find the skill deficit, empowering us to revise or make a plan of action to teach needed skill sets for better task completion.

RELATED SKILL SETS YOU MAY WISH TO EXPLORE WITH THE CHILDREN:

- Applying Past Knowledge
- Cognitive Flexibility
- Cognitive Persistence
- Critical Thinking
- Decision-Making
- Planning
- Previewing

- Prioritizing
- Problem-Solving
- Project Planning
- Sequencing
- Successive Processing
- Task Management

WHAT'S UNDERNEATH WORKSHEET

Expected behavior: _____

Clearly Defined Tasks

1. _____

2. _____

3. _____

4. _____

5. _____

Executive functions related to each task:

1. _____

2. _____

3. _____

Where are the skill deficits?

1. _____

2. _____

3. _____

4. _____

5. _____

What's the specific plan for building the needed skill?

1. _____

2. _____

3. _____

4. _____

5. _____

What are the support skills needed?

1. _____

2. _____

3. _____

4. _____

5. _____

How are we going to know this specific skill is improving?

1. _____

2. _____

3. _____

4. _____

5. _____

Thinking

THE FLASHLIGHT TECHNIQUE

DESCRIPTION: The Flashlight Technique is based on the work of cognitive scientist J.P. Das, co-author of *Assessment of Cognitive Processes: The Pass Theory of Intelligence,* and neurologist Frederic Perez-Alvarez and educational psychologist Carme Timoneda-Gallart, authors of *A Better Look at Intelligent Behavior.*

Children with inattention often wish to be on-task, but they have difficulty re-alerting to the desired stimuli after their brains drift off and attend to something else. We can kindly help the child become attuned to their "Re-Alerting Engine" by teaching her that, in her mind, there is a flashlight. The flashlight can be turned on to alert them to a specific stimulus; it can be shined on that stimulus to "focus." When children are empowered to focus on what they need to and even re-alert and re-focus after their minds drift, then they are better able to control their attention.

RELATED SKILL SETS YOU MAY WISH TO EXPLORE WITH THE CHILDREN:

- Alerting Attention
- Cognitive Flexibility
- Cognitive Persistence
- Focused Attention
- Impulse Control

- Planning
- Previewing
- Prioritizing
- Sustained Attention
- Working Memory

LET'S PLAY:

Talk with the child one-on-one in a kind, collaborative manner and tell him that you have been noticing he has difficulty keeping his attention focused on the work in class. Ask him if he has noticed as well. Then share that you have an idea that might help. Tell him that you once had a student named Max who taught you about imaginary flashlights. Max said that when his mind was drifting in class and he would catch himself, he would switch on an imaginary flashlight and point it where he needed to be focusing.

Ask the child if he thinks this might be helpful and talk with him about how you can help with questions and cuing prompts in class. Agree to the prompts, so that he feels helped and supported, not humiliated, in class. That's it; super simple. A kind conversation, a social narrative story and a plan the two of you develop together to help him learn how to alert, focus and sustain his attention.

The Components of the Flashlight Technique:

1. Helping the child become more aware of his own "attention engine." What does he focus on? What draws his attention? How does he know what he is supposed to focus on? How does he know when a person, place or thing is important to focus on?

2. Helping the child become aware of the process of "drift." When does his attention shift? When does he drift off? What is he thinking about or noticing when he drifts?

3. Helping the child to "re-alert" his attention so that he is no longer in "drift"; instead he is actively seeking a relevant stimulus upon which to focus.

4. Helping the child to "re-engage" with the salient stimulus, usually a person, topic, task or activity.

Teach how to "Begin to Notice." Raising the child's' awareness level of what it feels like to be on- or off-task is the first step. I liken it to imagining he is a rocket ready to blast off into space. His job is to notice if his "alertness engine" is in the on or off position. What is he attending to? What is he supposed to be attending to?

1. Help him notice and write down how his thoughts, posture or behaviors change when he has shifted to the "off-task" position to aid in his self-correction.

2. Help him make a plan to catch himself "on-task." Noticing what is helping him remain on-task empowers him.

3. Help him be mindfully aware of where his "attention flashlight" is pointing.

4. Once he is in the habit of noticing, he is in a position to implement his re-alerting strategies.

Teach how to "Re-Alert." The mind drifts off, seeking new stimuli to keep it alert. The challenge is that now the student is alert to something that is off-task or has little to do with the topic, task or lesson. The key is to help the child re-alert to what is salient to his learning. Use kind cuing, questions and prompts. "Sammy, what do you think about (the current topic)…" "Sammy, can you take a moment to think about (an aspect of the current topic) and tell me in a few minutes what you think?"

Teach how to "Re-Engage." Once the child is aware and is re-alert and focused on the relevant task, now he can re-engage with the work. His strategy is to shine his pretend flashlight on the person or task to which he needs to attend, then direct his "attention energy" toward that person or task.

CUING A CHILD WITH INATTENTION

The Flashlight Technique Cuing Questions

1. Teaching the child to notice he is off-task.

   Q: Where is your flashlight pointing?

2. Helping him alert his brain to salient information.

   Q: Where does your flashlight need to point?

3. Helping the child push the re-engage button.

   Q: Can you let me know in a minute what you think about (current topic)?

Help the child to turn his flashlight on the person, topic or task, by respectfully asking him to reflect and be mindfully present regarding the current topic. Provide support, respect and encouragement to the student for his efforts.

Practice the Flashlight Technique in various settings and under different circumstances. Ask the student to come back and tell you the story of what worked and what needs revision.

Activity #22

Thinking
GROUP STORY

DESCRIPTION: The Group Story activity is a group game that encourages students to listen with attention and control their impulses to blurt out. It encourages cognitive flexibility, social or collaborative decision-making and applying rules and skills to a task.

RELATED SKILL SETS YOU MAY WISH TO EXPLORE WITH THE CHILDREN:

- Alerting Attention
- Applying Past Knowledge
- Cognitive Flexibility
- Cognitive Persistence
- Creative Thinking
- Critical Thinking
- Decision-Making
- Emotional Regulation

- Exploration
- Impulse Control
- Planning
- Previewing
- Prioritizing
- Problem-Solving
- Sequencing
- Successive Processing

MATERIALS: White board and dry erase marker, or paper and pen.

OPTIONAL: story cubes, picture cards, pre-written sentences to help students think of ideas for the story.

READY: The facilitator explains the directions to the students. Sitting in a circle so that each group member can see each other is helpful. The facilitator says, "I am going to give you the first sentence of a story. Next, we go clockwise so that the person to my left goes next. When it's your turn, you may add (1–3) sentences to this story. The rules are that the story must have a logical flow – you can change the elements of it, but it must make sense as a coherent, unified story. Group members are not allowed to say critical or negative things about another person's sentences. We must support each other's ideas with kindness while also contributing our own. We will discuss how the story turned out at the end. The person who goes last will create a concluding (1–3) sentence(s) that ends the story." The facilitator will either write down what each student says, or assign recorders to do the writing.

Intro to Story: Three sentences created by the facilitator that set up a scene.

Example:

1. Johnny came to school feeling tired.
2. When he sat down for morning meeting, he noticed that his friend, Bobby, was sitting with Charlie today.
3. Johnny felt sad about that.

The next group member contributes three sentences and so on until the story is complete.

REVIEW: The facilitator helps the group think about their thinking.

1. Was it difficult when someone changed the direction of the story in a way that was different than you imagined it would be?
2. Was it interesting to see how the story turned out?
3. Has anyone in the group had a feeling like Johnny had in the story?
4. Was what we thought might happen helpful to how Johnny felt?
5. How would your story have been different from the group story?

Activity #23

Thinking

PICTURE THIS – I'M ORGANIZED!

DESCRIPTION: Picture this is a visual reminder strategy for planning ahead.

RELATED SKILL SETS YOU MAY WISH TO EXPLORE WITH THE CHILDREN:

- Critical Thinking
- Decision-Making
- Inhibition
- Memory Strategy
- Planning

- Previewing
- Prioritizing
- Problem-Solving
- Visual Scanning
- Working Memory

MATERIALS: A camera, usual school materials and a method of printing a photograph.

READY: "Okay, we are going to use a visual reminder strategy for what you need to take home from school every day in order to successfully remember what you need."

LET'S PLAY:

1. Take a photograph of the essential materials that the student must bring home every day. Example: a photo of the Daily Planner, textbook(s) and pencil case. Take a separate photo for each subject if necessary.
2. Print the photos out and label them "Essentials," and then by subject.
3. Secure copies of the photos in the child's locker or binder or other place where they must return to at the end of the school day.
4. Ask the child to look at the pictures at the end of the day and make sure everything in the photos is in their backpack to take home.

REVIEW:

1. So how did we do?
2. Was looking at a photograph more helpful than a written checklist?
3. Was it a quicker way to remember your materials?

Activity #24

Thinking

COLOR NUMBER JUMP AROUND

DESCRIPTION: Color Number Jump Around is a game in which a child will use visual scanning and motor skills to make decisions about which spot to jump to on the floor. The child must use impulse control to inhibit impulsive choices in order to succeed at the game.

RELATED SKILL SETS YOU MAY WISH TO EXPLORE WITH THE CHILDREN:

- Inhibition
- Impulse Control
- Planning
- Previewing

- Prioritizing
- Problem-Solving
- Rhythm
- Sustained Attention

MATERIALS: Colored paper, masking tape, colored markers.

READY: The facilitator will tape different colored pieces of paper on the floor into a table grid with pages close enough together that a child could hop from one spot to the other. The grid should look like this:

Blue paper - 1	Yellow paper - 4	White paper - C
White paper - B	Green paper - 3	Red paper - 2
Red paper - D	Blue paper - A	Yellow paper - 5

LET'S PLAY: Ask the child to hop from 1–5 in order, try to not skip a number and hop as quickly as (s)he can without skipping any. Ask the child to hop from A–D. Ask the child to switch and hop like this: 1, A, 2, B, 3, C, 4, D, 5. Next, ask the child to hop in backwards numbers order, and backwards letter order. The facilitator can also create patterns by colors of paper. Each time, start the stopwatch.

REVIEW:

1. How difficult did it seem?

2. Did the timer make it more or less difficult?

3. What did you have to do in order to be successful?

4. What happened when you hopped on the wrong spot accidentally – what happened that caused the mistake?

5. Go over the "look, stop and think before you act" procedure with the child, encouraging the child to pause a moment before (s)he acts.

Activity #25

Thinking
STOP AND THINK FORTUNE TELLER

DESCRIPTION: A fun way to show children how to think about possible outcomes or consequences of choices.

RELATED SKILL SETS YOU MAY WISH TO EXPLORE WITH THE CHILDREN:

- Alerting Attention
- Cognitive Flexibility
- Cognitive Persistence
- Creative Thinking
- Emotional Regulation
- Exploration
- Focused Attention

- Impulse Control
- Inhibition
- Memory Strategy
- Sequencing
- Sustained Attention
- Visual Scanning

MATERIALS: Paper, scissors, pen, optional stickers.

INSTRUCTIONS:

Predicting your future using paper fortune tellers was a common pastime during the grade school years. Sometimes called "cootie catchers," paper fortune tellers magically told who liked you, who hated you, if you would be rich someday, and even answered questions. For our purposes, we will make a paper fortune teller to show us the possible consequences of our choices and how impulsive choices usually don't end up helping us achieve our desired results.

1. Create a perfect square of paper by folding the top left corner of a standard sheet of paper diagonally to the opposite side of the paper. Cut the excess strip off the bottom, open the folded sheet and you should have a square of paper measuring approximately 8 1/2 inches by 8 1/2 inches.

2. Refold the paper on the diagonal, but this time create the fold using the right, top corner folded over to the left bottom corner. Open the paper back to its square shape and you should have two crease marks running from corner to corner.

3. Grab a corner of the square and fold it to the center of the paper. Repeat for each corner until you have a smaller square of paper with four flaps.

4. Turn the paper over and again fold each corner into the middle to create an even smaller square with four flaps.

5. Turn the paper over again so that the four square flaps are facing up. Fold the paper in half along the open flap lines to create creases. The paper creases form a plus sign, since you are folding from side to side, not corner to corner.

6. Grab the fortune teller and open it up to try it. To open, use your index finger and thumb of your right hand under the square flaps on the right side. Do the same for the left side. Slowly bring your fingers together and the fortune teller will open.

7. Open and close the flaps on the fortune teller by opening and closing your fingers together, manipulating the flaps one way and then another.

8. Write four colors on the top, square flaps. Choose colors with different numbers of letters in the word, such as red (3), blue (4), green (5), orange (6). The flaps can be colored or decorated to match their respective colors.

9. Flip the fortune teller over and write eight possible behavior choices with numbers on the triangular flaps. Use one odd and one even number for each pair of flaps.

10. Raise the triangular flaps and write one fortune under each 1/2 triangle. Fortunes will vary depending on the age of the person making the fortune teller. Fortunes should help the facilitator teach the most likely consequence of the behavior choice.

11. Tell someone's fortune. Hold the fortune teller in your hand and have them choose a color. Open and close the device one time for each letter in the color. Next, have them choose a number and then open and close the fortune teller the correct number of times, based on their number. Finally, have them choose one more number, lift the selected flap, and read the fortune.

Activity #26

Thinking
BASEBALL SHARE AND TELL

DESCRIPTION: Baseball Share and Tell is a great way to review a social-emotional or psycho-educational lesson.

RELATED SKILL SETS YOU MAY WISH TO EXPLORE WITH THE CHILDREN:

- Applying Past Knowledge
- Creative Thinking
- Critical Thinking
- Decision-Making
- Emotional Regulation

- Exploration
- Impulse Control
- Narrative Language
- Problem-Solving
- Reflection

MATERIALS: 4 chairs and an object for "Home Plate."

READY: The facilitator goes over a quick review of a social-emotional lesson the group has learned previously. The facilitator creates questions on index cards related to the lesson and designed to get students thinking, remembering, and applying knowledge in order to answer them correctly.

LET'S PLAY: Divide the group into two teams. If there is an odd number, one child can be a scorekeeper and write on the board. That child can also be a "phone a friend pinch hitter" for either team who will be passed a question that the player at bat cannot answer. Team 1 lines up behind home plate. The facilitator asks the first child a question and if (s)he answers correctly, (s)he moves to first base. If a child answers incorrectly, (s)he must go to the end of the line. Play continues until there are three outs. If a child scores a run because he answers the first question right and his teammates answer three more correctly, a tally mark is placed on the board and the child sits down. If there are not three outs after all the children on a team have had a turn, those who missed their first question get another chance to answer one. When the team has made three outs, the other team gets a turn to play.

REVIEW: After each hit or strike out, the facilitator makes sure to fill gaps in understanding or to expand on previously learned material. This game is a fun way to review and assess student understanding.

Thinking
FIND "IT"
(FIND THE LEADER)

DESCRIPTION: Find "It" is a quick, energizing activity to help children become more alert, look for nonverbal cues and pay attention to peers. It is a fun activity you can use as a movement or brain break before a thinking or learning activity.

RELATED SKILL SETS YOU MAY WISH TO EXPLORE WITH THE CHILDREN:

- Alerting Attention
- Applying Past Knowledge
- Critical Thinking
- Decision-Making
- Emotional Regulation
- Exploration

- Focused Attention
- Impulse Control
- Problem-Solving
- Sustained Attention
- Visual Scanning

MATERIALS: Comfortable clothing.

READY: Have the children sit or stand in a circle. One student, whose turn it is, will be "IT" and stands in the middle of the circle and covers his/her eyes while the facilitator quietly chooses a leader who stays in his/her place.

LET'S PLAY: Once the leader is selected, "It" can open his or her eyes. Then the leader starts the game by nodding his head, reaching his arms up, or making circles with his hands and everyone follows his lead. Caution the children not to look directly at the leader or to indicate who the leader is when "It" uncovers his/her eyes. The child who is "It" turns slowly around, trying to figure out who the leader is. The leader should try to change actions when "It" is not looking at him. "It" gets three guesses. If "It" does not guess correctly, the leader becomes the new "It." If he guesses correctly, choose two other children to be the leader and "It."

REVIEW:

1. So how did we do?
2. What were the best clues to who IT was?
3. What made it difficult to notice?
4. How did the group do not looking directly at the leader?
5. Which impulses were more difficult to control: looking at the leader? Helping IT by giving clues? Laughing?

Great Work Kids,
We are learning to pay attention and think before we decide!

Activity
#28

Thinking
THE SCRIPT

DESCRIPTION: This is a follow-the-directions creative game to help students relax and have some fun before tuning into an academic challenge.

RELATED SKILL SETS YOU MAY WISH TO EXPLORE WITH THE CHILDREN:

- Alerting Attention
- Critical Thinking
- Decision-Making
- Emotional Regulation
- Exploration
- Focused Attention
- Impulse Control
- Motor Planning

- Motor Sequencing
- Planning
- Previewing
- Prioritizing
- Problem-Solving
- Sequencing
- Successive Processing
- Sustained Attention

MATERIALS: Sequenced instructions written on slips of paper for each student to follow until the last student's turn.

READY: The facilitator creates a "script" of instructions on separate slips of paper, so that each student will have one that will lead to the next student's turn to follow his script of directions.

LET'S PLAY: The facilitator gives each child one sentence. The child must pay close attention to what the instruction says. For example, it could read, "Say 'It's going to be a great day!' in a happy, warm tone." The student who will go next will have a slip of paper that reads, "When you hear a student say, "It's going to be a great day," you will get up, flip the light switch from on to off to on again and then sit down." The next child will have the instruction, "When you see the lights flash on and off, you should stand up, raise your arms over your head and say 'reach for the stars' and then sit down." Another example might be, "When you hear the word 'Love' go to the board and write Love five times, then sit down." The next child will have directions that follow and so on. The facilitator has made up the instructions and created the movement and actions to play like dominoes until each student has followed an instruction that inspires the next.

REVIEW:

1. So how did we do?
2. How hard was it not to share what your slip of paper said?
3. What made it difficult?
4. Was it difficult to notice or hear the clue that you needed to follow your instruction next?
5. Did you feel relaxed before your turn, after, or both?

Thinking

THE SORT IT OUT STRATEGY – THINK, STRATEGIZE, OBSERVE, RESPOND

DESCRIPTION: There is an exploration strategy called SODA known to clinicians that is applied in many different ways. We like to use an adaptation of SODA to help children learn how to apply their cognitive skills in order to be deliberate or intentional in their actions. We call our adaptation SORT It Out. In this activity we provide a variety of situations and the children decide how they would "SORT It Out." Once the children have learned this strategy "SORTING something out" becomes a cue or keyword to apply a child's deliberation, problem-solving and decision-making skills. You will often hear us collaboratively say to kids, "Let's SORT this out."

RELATED SKILL SETS YOU MAY WISH TO EXPLORE WITH THE CHILDREN:

- Attention
- Decision-Making
- Impulse Control
- Narrative Language
- Problem-Solving
- Successive Processing

MATERIALS: Pen, paper, scenarios.

READY: Tell the client, student or class that you are going to play a decision-making game where the children are faced with a situation in which they have to Think, Strategize, Observe and Respond in a helpful manner. Tell them you are calling this activity "Sorting It Out." We often need to sort out what we think, feel and do in tough situation. "Sorting it Out" helps us think, plan and respond with intent.

LET'S PLAY: The facilitator asks the students to imagine that they are faced with a social decision-making challenge. They will read the situation and then as a group, dyad, family or individual, they will write down how to SORT out the challenge. They will write down what they think about the situation, what their strategy is for managing the situation, what they will be looking for or observing to see if their resolution is on the right track and how they will respond to any specific challenges they face in addressing the situation.

Write the mnemonics on the board and go through a situation with the client, student, family or group. Possible situations are listed below; you can also write your own. You can play many variations of this activity. You can have the children act out the scenarios, write their own or even practice responding in "unhelpful ways" that the other students can "correct." The possibilities are endless. We have done this activity with pen and paper, on an outdoor stage at a park and even in the lunchroom, acting out the challenges. Adapt away and enjoy the learning.

Examples of Social Decision Making Challenges

SCHOOL	FRIENDSHIP	SAFETY	PROBLEM-SOLVING	GROUPS
Someone in your class teased you because you got so many wrong on your spelling test.	Your friend is playing a game with someone else and it is only a two-player game.	Some boys were pushing you off the play set at recess.	A girl in class teased you about your clothes.	The table where you usually sit at lunch is full.
Your friends had finished their work but you hadn't. They were playing a game.	You noticed a new girl in class didn't have anyone to play with during recess.	You waited a long time, but your mom didn't come to pick you up after school.	On the playground, a boy kept chasing you. You didn't like it.	You are waiting for the doors to open with a group of kids who are talking to each other but not to you.
The teacher asks you a question. Everyone had their hands up, you don't know the answer.	You and friend were playing a game. Another classmate asked to join your game.	You were waiting to swing. When it was your turn, another child jumped in front of you and took the swing.	A kid on the playground yelled at you saying, "you are in the way of our game!"	You are a little late for a birthday party. Everyone is playing together and seems to ignore you.
You were talking, and a teacher scolded you for being noisy. You didn't know you were being loud.	You friend was shooting baskets in PE class and missed every shot. The others kids laughed and said, "he stinks."	An older kid threatened to punch you if you didn't get off the playground.	When you lined up for recess, the person behind you kept pushing you.	You had a fight with your best friend and you aren't talking right now. Your other friends don't know if they should take sides.

Activity
#30

Thinking

I CAN SEE
CLEARLY NOW

DESCRIPTION: Remember that old song, "I can see clearly now, the rain is gone. I can see all obstacles in my way?" In this activity, we play with a group of images, the rain clouds and sun, to help children look at a problem or experience in a new way. We cut out the sun, rain and clouds and let the child move them around on the table or in the workspace to tell the following story. The story sentences are prompts to inspire exploration. You might offer some other sentences or allow the child to tell the story in a manner that is meaningful to him. The goal is exploration of his thoughts, feeling, obstacles and even distortions or "changeable beliefs" about the problem, person or life experience.

RELATED SKILL SETS YOU MAY WISH TO EXPLORE WITH THE CHILDREN:

- Cognitive Flexibility

- Emotional Regulation

- Exploration

- Narrative Language

- Problem-Solving

- Reflection

I CAN SEE CLEARLY NOW WORKSHEET

One day I had a problem, the problem was _____.

Experiencing that problem made me feel _____.

I thought I'd look at the parts of my problem and figure out if I could see it a new way.

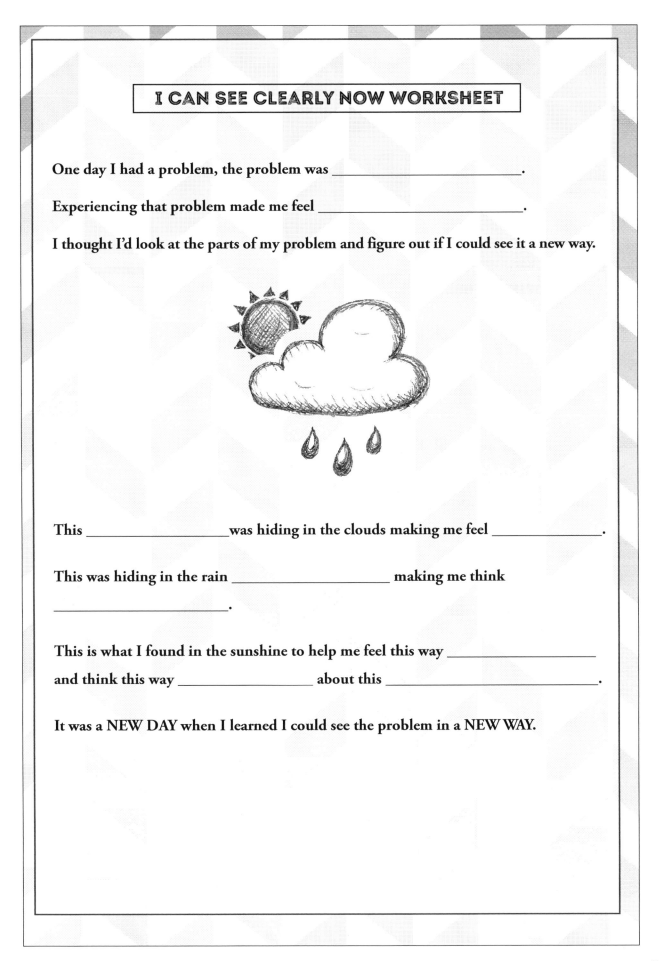

This _____ was hiding in the clouds making me feel _____.

This was hiding in the rain _____ making me think

_____.

This is what I found in the sunshine to help me feel this way _____

and think this way _____ about this _____.

It was a NEW DAY when I learned I could see the problem in a NEW WAY.

113

Activity #31

Thinking
MY ATTENTION ENGINE

DESCRIPTION: Another way we make some of the executive functions "transparent" to help children understand, in age-appropriate terms, how their brain works is to tell them that everyone has an attention engine. It's like a beautiful colorful train that has different cars, responsible for different parts of our attention cycle. In this activity, we draw and color the different boxcars that make up our "Attention Engine," then we can talk and analyze different experiences by writing in each box car what parts of our attention were active each moment of the experience.

Attention Engine #1
EXPRESS

For further exploration, use this fill-in-the-blank story or write your own to explore specific situations with the child or student to help him become more aware of his attention engine, how it works and what he'd like to improve in order to pay better attention to what is important for his well-being.

MY ATTENTION ENGINE WORKSHEET

My Attention Engine looks like _____.

My Attention Engine turns on when _____.

My Attention Engine is going along fine when _____.

My Attention Engine is super bored when _____.

My Attention Engine is sleeping when _____.

One day, My Attention Engine was_____. It felt like

_____. I was having fun when_____. But then I knew

I needed to _____. It was hard when _____.

So I chose to _____. It really helped when

_____. Now I know how to _____. This

is what made my Attention Engine work better _____.

Write your own story with fill-in-the-blanks and discuss what helps your Attention
Engine work best.

Activity #32

Thinking
FINGER THINKING

DESCRIPTION: Finger Thinking is a tangible way to help children be aware of what part of the attention cycle they are in at this given moment. Ask the child to hold up her hand and spread out her fingers. Tell her that her fingers can help her to be aware of what part of her Attention Engine is active at any moment. Show her that her pointer finger turns her engine on, her second finger chooses where to focus and her third finger sends her focused energy to the target. Show her that she can place her hand on her thigh or desk or another quiet place to help remind her to be alert and intentional.

Now, when she gets off task or catches herself in "drift," she can simply put her hand flat on her thigh and push her pointer finger gently against her leg to rev up her engine, push her second finger gently against her leg to remind her to choose a relevant target of her attention and push her third finger gently against her leg to remind her to direct her focused energy toward the target. This easy-to-learn "1-2-3 Rev up, aim and focus" reminder process is helpful when children drift. It is a tangible way for the child to say to herself, "I am aware that I drifted." "I am taking action to re-alert and re-attend."

Finger Thinking can be used for other reminders, as well, the child with whom you work might be able to generate some other great ideas too.

"I can remind myself to breathe." "1-2-3 Breathe."

"I can remind myself to calm down." "1-2-3 Choose Calm."

"I can remind myself to replace this negative thought with a positive thought." "1-2-3 Be Positive."

"I can remind myself to plan out my actions." "1-2-3 Make A Plan."

"I can rev up my engine to . . ." "1-2-3 Wake Up."

"I can focus my energy on . . ." "1-2-3 Get Energized"

"I can direct my energy toward . . ." "1-2-3 Be Purposeful." And so on…

Thinking
WHOSE JELLY BEANS AM I HOLDING?

DESCRIPTION: There are times in life when we have feelings that are more related to what is going on for someone else than they are related to our own thoughts or experiences. Particularly when we are dependent on another person, such as a parent or teacher, we might experience the weight of their needs and desires, causing us some discomfort. It's helpful for children to have the awareness that their feelings, particularly worry, anger, frustration, fear or distress, might be about someone else, not themselves. Providing an activity to help children sort out what is about them and what is about the other person benefits them immensely. In our work, we call bearing the weight of someone else's wants, needs, experiences, thoughts or feelings "Holding Their Jelly Beans." When you are "holding someone else's jelly beans" you are carrying their feelings, thoughts or concerns. There are times when this awareness allows the child to put down the other person's jelly beans, so they can get back to the authenticity of carrying their own.

RELATED SKILL SETS YOU MAY WISH TO EXPLORE WITH THE CHILDREN:

- Cognitive Flexibility

- Emotional Regulation

- Exploration

- Narrative Language

- Problem-Solving

- Reflection

Reflecting on My Authentic Feelings

What is bothering me? _____

What am I upset about? _____

What are my current feelings? _____

Who else feels this way? _____

Are my feelings a response to someone else's feelings? _____

What or who am I responding to? _____

Might I be holding someone else's jelly beans? _____

LET ME EXAMINE MY FEELINGS WORKSHEET

How I feel: _____

Why I feel this way: _____

These are my jelly beans

1. _____
2. _____
3. _____
4. _____

These are the other person's jelly beans

1. _____
2. _____
3. _____
4. _____

These are the jelly beans I am holding

1. _____
2. _____
3. _____
4. _____

These are the jelly beans I need to let go of

1. _____
2. _____
3. _____
4. _____

This is what I am going to think, in order to put the other person's jelly beans down.

_____

This is what I am going to say, in order to put the other person's jelly beans down.

_____

If I decide to talk it out with the other person, this is how I am going to politely ask

the other person to hold their own jelly beans. _____

These are the signs I am going to look for next time to help me be aware that I might
be holding someone else's jelly beans.

1. _____   2. _____

3. _____   4. _____

Activity #34

Thinking
PUT A BOW ON IT

DESCRIPTION: When children are learning how to sequence activities, that is, understand that there is a beginning, middle and end to each activity, you can teach them how to explore tasks, activities and experiences by drawing or writing out what they do in which order. For example, when we draw something, we pick up the marker, draw the picture, then put the marker back. When we play with a toy, we choose the toy, play with the toy, then put it back. Initiating actions such as play is fun and rewarding. Yet sometimes completing an action is interrupted by distractions, such as other thoughts, interests or people. Getting into the habit of completing what one started is important to both academic and behavioral success. A helpful way to help children complete actions is to teach them that, after they complete the third step of an activity, they can "wrap a bow on it," meaning that the action is complete and they can move onto the next action.

This worksheet helps children to sequence an activity and tie a bow on it. Once the children have done this a few times, the term "Wrap a bow on it" comes to mean let's complete this activity by doing the last part of the action so we can move on to our next activity. "Let's wrap a bow on that," signals to the child that the last piece of the action is still waiting for them to complete.

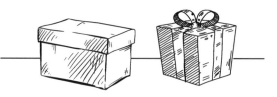

My activity or task is: _____

The first part of the action is: _____

The second part of the action is: _____

The last part of the action is : _____

I'll wrap a bow on it when the task, action or activity is completed.

While everything we do can be broken down into the first, second and third actions we take, remember that some larger tasks may need more sequences of three parts of actions. There have been times when we are sequencing activities such as hygiene routines, homework routines and even, "How to make a sandwich," where we draw series of three boxes on the floor, table or marker board to help the children see *how many action sequences* are often needed when we scaffold a task. Sequencing is one of the most important executive functions, when children learn how to sequence parts of actions, they are better organizers, planners, communicators and task completers.

Activity #35

Thinking
I'LL GIVE THIS 10

DESCRIPTION: There are many times in life when we have "BIG feelings," as Wendy Young of Kidlutions says. How we cope with and manage those feelings affects how we learn, behave and get along with others. Having a helpful cognitive strategy to cope with strong feelings makes all the difference. In I'll Give This 10, we explain to the children that experiencing feelings is an important part of life. When we experience our feelings, we can feel them fully, yet we need to be able to metabolize our feelings so that we can move through them and not get stuck in them. Allowing yourself to feel and then move through a feeling is what makes you a robust person. We want to feel our emotions; we just don't want to be prisoners of them.

In I'll Give This 10, we learn how to recognize that when we are having BIG feelings, we name them and then tell ourselves how long we plan to experience these BIG feelings. We usually choose to "feel our emotions" for 10 seconds, 10 minutes, or 10 hours. Of course, this "rule of 10" is a cognitive construct, it could be 2 minutes or 27 minutes. But children get "10," so it is a wonderful starting point to help a child to determine:

1. "HOW BIG is this feeling?" and
2. "HOW LONG am I going to let this feeling determine my thoughts and behaviors?"

Let's explore a few examples to get you thinking about how this suits the children with whom you work or teach.

a. If you waited in line for an ice cream cone and when it's finally your turn, you learn they are out of vanilla ice cream, you might say to yourself, "That is super frustrating. I was so hungry for a vanilla cone. I'll give this 10 seconds and then ask for a chocolate one."

b. If you get dressed to go surfing with your mom, then learn that she planned a day at the zoo, you can say to yourself, "I'd much rather go surfing. I'm gonna feel disappointed for 10 minutes, then I'm gonna think about which animals I want to see at the zoo."

c. If you get mad at your dad because he won't let you go on a holiday with your best friend, you might tell yourself, "I am so upset! I have a right to my feelings. I'm gonna stew in this one for a while. I'm gonna give this 10 hours, then I'm going to let it go."

Self-Regulation Calming and Alerting Activities

While we have shared thoughts and ideas up to this point primarily about cognition, how we think, how we shift our thoughts and how we can build higher-functioning children with better thinking and social-interactive skills, there remains much to say about self-regulation. Although a lot of our work focuses on improving children's cognition, self-regulation in many ways precedes cognition. If we are not calm, well-modulated and balanced in our emotional states, our cognition suffers. Therefore, the next section of activities are those you can use to either calm or alert the brain and body. As we have stated earlier, whether an activity is calming or alerting, in large part, is an individual difference. Some of these activities might calm some children and alert others. Some are designed to help children "get their energy out"; others are designed to "calm their energy down." Still others are designed for musical, motor or feelings exploration.

Self-Regulation
FEELINGS HIDE AND SEEK

DESCRIPTION: Feelings Hide and Seek is a combination of a scavenger hunt and hide and seek. The object of the activity is to control the impulse to peek, to use self-regulation to follow the rules, and to recognize and describe an emotion.

RELATED SKILL SETS YOU MAY WISH TO EXPLORE WITH THE CHILDREN:

- Alerting Attention
- Cognitive Flexibility
- Cognitive Persistence
- Creative Thinking
- Critical Thinking
- Decision-Making

- Emotional Regulation
- Exploration
- Narrative Language
- Visual Scanning
- Working Memory

MATERIALS: Index cards, tape, pen.

READY: The facilitator says, "We are going to play a game that is a cross between a prize hunt and hide and seek! While we play, we are going to learn about recognizing our impulses and using self-control to follow the rules."

Ask the children to write down a difficult or unhappy feeling or emotion word on an index card. The children should mention their choices so that there are no duplicates and the facilitator should add some feelings to the bunch as well. Before writing, the group can brainstorm a list together.

LET'S PLAY: Once each child has written an emotion word on a card, the facilitator says, "Feelings are neither good nor bad – they are just human! But because they can feel good or bad while we have them, it is what we do with the feeling that is important. Here are the rules of this game: Each of you will have a turn to take one of these feeling cards and hide it by sticking it with tape someplace in the room. You may not hide it inside or underneath anything. It should be a place that's hard to notice but in plain sight. While the hider is sticking his/her card someplace, the rest of you will close your eyes and cover them with your hands. You may notice that you have a strong impulse to peek. I want you to notice if you do have that impulse to tell yourself that you will not – think of a strategy that will help, like counting in your head, taking deep breaths, or thinking of something wonderful. If I see anyone peeking, they must skip a turn."

"When the hider sits back down, I will say 'ready' and you may open your eyes. When I say 'okay go' you will be able to walk around the room and look for the card. You may feel an impulse to run, but I want you to again use self-control to slow down and walk. If I notice someone is running, they will have to sit back down for 1 minute or until the card is found. Whoever finds the card gets to read it aloud and share a time either when someone might feel that way or when they themselves have felt that way. Then, we will brainstorm together some things a person can do to move on from that feeling and feel better. The reader will write all of our ideas on the back of the card in note form. If you find more than one card on the first round, you must choose someone else to read who hasn't gone yet."

REVIEW:

1. Have you ever had a time when you felt this way? What helped you?
2. On a scale of 1–10, how difficult is this feeling? How difficult is the situation you described?
3. What could someone try if they are feeling this way that might help?

When the all the feeling cards have been found and possible coping strategies have been written on the back, use a hole punch to put a ring through the cards. Now you have a set of coping strategies for difficult feelings! Kids love this group game!

Activity #2

Self-Regulation
FREEZE DANCE

DESCRIPTION: A movement game that helps children think about body control and inhibition of moment while using their memories.

During Freeze Dance, children dance to music while the facilitator holds up a picture of a stick figure in a certain bodily position or posture. The facilitator should hold the picture up for 15–90 seconds, depending on the age of the children. The children are asked to observe the picture while dancing and moving around in their own way. When the music stops, the children should get into the position that was in the picture. Children must exercise self-control by stopping their bodies when the music stops, and follow directions. Children must also use memory skills to remember the stick figure position and recreate it in themselves when the music stops.

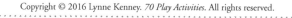

Self-Regulation
SUN SALUTATION

DESCRIPTION: Sun Salutation is a series of three yoga moves that are done in a specific sequence three times in a row for calming. It takes 6–10 minutes to do them, depending on how fast you move. We use these with our students to help them calm before tests; they can also be used whenever a child feels rushed, impulsive or stressed out.

RELATED SKILL SETS YOU MAY WISH TO EXPLORE WITH THE CHILDREN:

- Balance
- Cognitive Flexibility
- Coordination
- Emotional Regulation
- Focused Attention
- Impulse Control

- Inhibition
- Motor Management
- Motor Planning
- Motor Sequencing
- Sustained Attention

MATERIALS: Comfortable clothing.

READY: Tell the child that sometimes, if our brains or bodies are racing, we can slow down by standing in place and doing a few simple movements that are fun and relaxing. "Have you ever done a Sun Salutation? Let's give it a try."

LET'S PLAY: "We're going to do a sequence of three yoga moves that we may find relaxing. After we do this sequence a few times, you can make up your own. Then you can be the teacher."

"We will do this dynamic yoga stretch three times in a row. The third time is super calming, as the body and brain have had time to work together letting go of thought and relaxing into the movement."

1. "Start with your feet shoulder width apart. In *70 Play Activities*, we call that ready position. Standing up tall, hands are at your sides, your head is aligned with your spine, you are relaxed."

2. "Now raise your arms from the sides of your body reaching like the sun, all the way up over your head. See, you just made a sun. As we lift our arms, we breathe deeply in and then out."

3. "Now we bend forward at our waists and put our hands on the floor; we're about to do a downward dog. You can bend your knees a little if that feels more comfortable. Keep breathing deeply and blowing that air out. In *70 Play Activities*, we call this taking our BIG breaths."

4. "Now that we are bent over, we will walk our hands forward while we press our shoulders toward our knees. See, there you have it – downward dog! Good job."

5. "Now we'll let our knees move to the floor so we can round our backs like cats and then flatten them like cows. We round and flatten three times. Feel your body relaxing as you take BIG breaths."

6. "Very nice, now we'll roll our toes under so we can pop back up into downward dog, pushing our shoulders toward our knees to feel a nice deep stretch."

7. "Finally we'll roll back onto our heels, letting our bodies hang, then we'll roll up our spines to a standing position super slowly."

8. "Now that we are standing we begin again with a beautiful big huge sun salutation stretch, a BIG breath and we'll do the sequence again. Ready? Okay, let's go."

9. "Sun salutation to downward dog, three cat cows, a roll back to downward dog and we'll finish with sun salutation."

10. "Do you want to say the words so we know what to do or shall I?"

REVIEW

1. How did that feel?

2. What did you like about our Sun Salutation sequence?

3. Which part did you like best?

4. What felt more difficult? Anything?

5. Did you like doing it three times? Would you have wanted to do it again?

6. When you feel like you need to slow down or calm down, how could you use this sequence to help you?

7. Would you like to make up your own sequence?

8. We can do the Sun Salutation a few times when we meet and then you might be ready to make up your own.

Activity
#4

Self-Regulation
MOUNTAIN CLIMBER BLAST-OFFS

DESCRIPTION: It can be helpful to have an alerting activity that takes about a minute to help clients or students raise the oxygen levels in their bodies in order to become more alert. Mountain Climber Blast-Offs are fast and furious and they make kids wake up and even laugh. They are best used with children who are able to stay calm and not become over-exhilarated and then impulsive. So create structure for the activity; tell them exactly what you are alerting them to do and tell them clearly what action to take immediately after they are done.

RELATED SKILL SETS YOU MAY WISH TO EXPLORE WITH THE CHILDREN:

- Balance
- Cognitive Persistence
- Coordination
- Emotional Regulation
- Focused Attention

- Impulse Control
- Motor Management
- Motor Planning
- Motor Sequencing

MATERIALS: Comfortable clothing.

READY: "Alright, looks like you all need a little wake-up call. Let's do a minute of Mountain Climber Blast-Offs. Remember, you're like a Navy Seal – stay focused and keep your body in control. We have serious work ahead of us and we need to bring our bodies to full "attention.""

LET'S PLAY: "Whether this is your first time or your 100th, Mountain Climber Blast-Offs build better bodies and more focused brains. We'll walk you through it one time to make sure you Navy Seals know how to do 'em, then you have one minute to do as many as you can." (If you have a student who has done these a bunch of times before, let him or her lead, the kids love taking turns being the teacher.)

1. "We stand in ready position. Standing up tall, hands are at your sides, your head is aligned with your spine, you are relaxed."

2. "Then it's three swift moves, bend over to the floor hands shoulder width apart, feet close to your hands, jump those feet back so that you are in push-up position, and bend the elbows. We call out "One" on the bend over, "Two" on the feet back and "Three" on the elbows bent. Now you are ready for three mountain climbers with each leg."

3. "Bring the right knee in towards the chest, resting the foot on the floor. Jump up and switch feet in the air, bringing the left foot in and the right foot back. Do this three times with each leg, then jump up to a stand."

4. "That's ONE! Wow! Are we really ready for this? OKAY, when I say go, you will do the mountain climber sequence as many times as possible in 60 seconds. When I say "Attention" you will pop up to READY POSITION and come to ATTENTION, looking forward with arms straight and tight along the sides of your body."

5. "Ready Go!"

REVIEW:

1. So how did we do?

2. Were you able to keep control of your body?

3. What part of the activity was easy?

4. Do you feel more alert and ready to learn?

5. Do you have ideas on what we/you could change next time to mix up the movements?

Activity #5

Self-Regulation
PENTATONIC PIANO

DESCRIPTION: The pentatonic scales are based on five notes per octave instead of the common seven notes per octave. Pentatonic scales are simpler and often found in folk and children's music. The pentatonic scales are a wonderful introductory level of music for children, as they are upbeat and easy to master.

Bobby McFerrin does a great video of pentatonic hopping on YouTube. Simply google Bobby McFerrin Power of the Pentatonic Scale. Watch it; you will laugh and smile. Our version is super simple and made for kids. We do it to alert the kids when they are getting distracted or bored in group therapy or in class. The kids love it; it's their favorite activity.

RELATED SKILL SETS YOU MAY WISH TO EXPLORE WITH THE CHILDREN:

- Alerting Attention
- Applying Past Knowledge
- Balance
- Cognitive Flexibility
- Cognitive Persistence
- Coordination
- Decision-Making
- Emotional Regulation
- Exploration

- Focused Attention
- Impulse Control
- Inhibition
- Motor Management
- Motor Planning
- Motor Sequencing
- Visual Scanning
- Working Memory

MATERIALS: Comfortable clothing; blue tape; gym shoes.

READY: Lay down a straight line of blue tape about 8 feet long. Now, every foot, lay a piece of blue tape perpendicular to the line so that you have a line with nine segments. Each of the segments is actually a musical note. Cool, eh? You can make this "Pentatonic Piano" on your own or involve the kids, it's a good planning, problem-solving and decision-making activity.

The notes in the scale of C, from left to right, are C D E G A. Now that you have laid down your "Pentatonic Piano" hop on C and make the Middle C sound. If you do not know what "Middle C" sounds like, listen online, it's easy to find videos on YouTube.

C….. Now hop on D. D……. Okay perfect, now you are you are ready to play.

"How many of you play the piano? Have you ever played the piano with your whole body? That's what we are about to do."

LET'S PLAY: Here is the wording we use. Because there is a lot of movement in this activity, use your judgment regarding pacing, words and timing. We love this activity. Have fun!!!

1. Stand up tall, with Middle C right in front of you. Now you are able to hop forward and hop back, playing one note at a time.

2. Hop forward on Middle C, then immediately backward.

3. You just played a note with your body, the note was Middle C.

4. Now hop on D, then immediately backward.

5. You just played D.

6. Now turn on some music and hop to the tunes.

7. When you have the hang of it, you can make up your own tunes or hop to your favorite songs. Hum along or ask your friend to hum while you hop, the Bobby McFerrin way.

8. See, you are a musician and you didn't even know it. There's more music to come, so keep your sneakers on.

REVIEW:

1. What did you notice about the individual notes?
2. Which notes did you like best?
3. What was fun? Hopping, listening to your friends make the sound as you hopped or writing your own music?
4. Now, have even more fun by listening to simple songs on sites like thekiboomers. com and play all your favorite old-time tunes. You can graduate to popular songs any time you are ready.

Self-Regulation
BE THE TREE

DESCRIPTION: Sometimes you will meet children who have not had the experience of centered calmness. They are often frenetic, moving with much energy. It's not easy to say to these children, "just sit; be still; stop moving." We need to begin with the movement and empower them to alter their speed, rate and volume of their movement so that they can actually experience calmness in a new way.

RELATED SKILL SETS YOU MAY WISH TO EXPLORE WITH THE CHILDREN:

- Alerting Attention
- Balance
- Coordination
- Creative Thinking
- Emotional Regulation
- Exploration
- Focused Attention

- Impulse Control
- Inhibition
- Motor Management
- Motor Planning
- Motor Sequencing
- Reflection

MATERIALS: Comfortable clothing.

READY: Tell the children "we are going to stand comfortably in ready position with our toes facing forward, our belly button pulled in and our shoulders calmly relaxed."

LET'S PLAY: "Let's stand up, feet forward, belly button in, knees over our feet, hips over our knees, shoulders; round up back and down. Now you are aligned. This helps your body to move naturally."

"Let's plant roots for our tree. Now you can move in the security of knowing you are firmly planted in the ground. Feel your tree moving from the roots, rocking back and forth. You can flex your knees or move your hips. Everyone is a different kind of tree. Simply be the kind of tree that you are."

"Now the wind is going to blow lightly at first, just creating a ripple in our leaves. We lift our rippling leaves up on our branches from our arms, as we feel the wonderful wind move our arms slowly making our leaves crinkle in the breeze."

"Oh, the breeze is picking up and it's becoming windy. Our branches are moving, our base is grounded in the earth. It remains firm, safe and secure. But our branches are moving, beginning to move wildly as our leaves are singing with the sound of the wind. We are a tree orchestra. And we shake and we tremor as the wind howls. It feels good to let our energy fly away with the wind. We are moving with the wind and our body is moved back and forth while our feet are firmly planted in the ground."

"Ohhh, now the breeze is slowly calming down and our leaves are coming to a rest. Our branches, as our arms, are slowing falling to our sides. Our bodies are becoming calm. The wind is calm. Our branches begin to rest; our leaves go back to sitting peacefully, laying on our branches. We are breathing out, feeling exhilarated now because we are calmed. Our rocking trunk is now resting. Still. We are at peace with our surroundings. We are now a tree that sits in silence, quiet and restful."

REVIEW:

1. What was it like to plant your roots firmly in the ground?

2. What kind of tree were you?

3. How did you imagine your leaves?

4. What did the wind feel like as it blew across the branches and crinkled your leaves.

5. How did the trunk of your tree feel?

6. What kind of energy were you experiencing?

7. Was there any moment when you thought that your tree might become unearthed or were you always firmly planted in the ground?

8. When you came back to a resting position, what sort of energy did you experience?

9. How did that feel?

GOOD WORK!

Activity #7

Self-Regulation
MIDDLE C O-H-M

DESCRIPTION: We call this activity Middle C Ohm. O-H-M as in Yoga. This is an activity that evolved out of my interaction with Musician for the Brain, Nacho Arimany. Nacho is a multi-instrumentalist who has a compelling methodology called **Elemental Sounds and Rhythms**, which maximizes the natural rhythms in our lives for better balance, harmony and productivity. Nacho is also the composer of inTime, the amazing listening program from Advanced Brain Technologies. One day, Nacho was showing me the difference in the feeling of resonance when you say "AAA" as compared with "OHM."

Years earlier, I had noticed when my daughter was about 6 months old and her tummy hurt, I would lay her across my legs and pat her back. She made this deeply resonant sound that sounded a lot like OHM. I could feel the vibration of her voice on my legs. It was clear to me that it was very soothing to her, but I didn't know why.

When Nacho was showing me the difference between "OHM," which is a deeply resonant sound, versus "AAA," which is almost an upper register sound, **I observed they felt very different**. It struck me that children would enjoy experiencing the difference in the sounds, so we made it like a game. And the children really enjoyed experiencing the difference in the feelings, actually the sensation, the bodily sensation between AAA and OHM.

LET'S PLAY:

So in this activity we **simply sit in a circle** with the children or sit across from the children in chairs or sit on the ground criss-cross style and say to them, "Let's play Middle C OHM." I am going to make some sounds and then you can imitate the sounds and then eventually you'll make those sounds and I'll imitate those sounds.

So let's just begin with what middle C sounds like. And then, if you have an app on your phone where you can play a middle C or you have a piano play the middle C. We just play the middle C and it goes "Laaaaaaaaa." That's what middle C sounds like, Laaaaaaaaaaaaa.

"So, now everyone say a middle C. Let's all do it together. Ready? 3, 2, 1. Laaaaaaaaaaaa. Great! Everyone did great! Now that we have done it, let's add a different consonant to it. What we are going to say is, 'Aaaaaaaaaaaaa.' Alright. So you are just producing a soft A – Aaaaaaaaaaaaa. Alright. Everyone, we are going to do it together. You ready? Aaaaaaaaaaaaaaa." And you can even have them put their hands out as though they are sending the sound to the universe, Aaaaaaaaaaaaaa. And then you close your fists, because that's how Nacho says that's the end of the note, everybody stop.

Now you play variations a little bit. You can do the short notes, long notes, you can count with your fingers. Aaaaaaaaaaaaa, two, three, four. Or just use your fingers. Aaaaaaaaaaaaa. Then you use your closed fists again, which is the Nacho sign for "that's the end of that note."

Next, you introduce the sound OHMmmmm. This is a more resonant sound; it comes from deep within the chest. You all experience the difference in the feeling with OHMmmmm, then you can even drop it down an octave, OHMmmmm.

For this activity, you are helping the children experience the difference between what is considered a head note, Aaaaaaaaaaaaaa, compared with a resonant note, OHMmmmm. You can use the magic piano app or visit thekiboomers.com for inspiration.

So that is Middle C Ohm. And you can do all sorts of things with it. You could make an orchestra out of it. **Have the children stand up and split the sounds among different groups**. Have them stand across from one another and alternate the sounds. You could use quarter notes, half notes or whole notes with the sounds as well. Aaaaaaaaaaaaaa. OHMmmmm. OHMmmmm. Aaaaaaaaaaaaaa. OHMmmmm. OHMmmmm. With these two simple sounds, you can play Middle C Ohm and the children will have an experience of themselves as musical.

ITSY-BITSY SPIDER

The itsy-bitsy spider
Climbed up the water spout

Down came the rain
And washed the spider out

Out came the sun
And dried up all the rain

And the itsy-bitsy spider
Climbed up the spout again

Activity #8

Self-Regulation
THE FAMILY ORCHESTRA

DESCRIPTION: The Family Orchestra is a wonderful way to break the ice in a classroom or in a family or with a group to turn everybody into a musical orchestra. It's not a very difficult thing to do and it's a whole lot of fun. **Here is what you say and how you do it**.

LET'S PLAY:

"So today we are going to see how musical everyone is. Let's do this. Let's split the room into four parts. You all in the front right section are going to be the pulse of our music. What you are going to do is stand up and march. One, two, three, four. One, two, three, four. So, can you stand up for a second and try that? Just stand up and march a nice big strong consistent beat. Terrific! Okay, you guys can sit down."

"Now, the right quarter group in the back. You all stand up; what you are going to do is be the la la. So you are going to say, la la; la la; la la; la la. Can you stand up and try it? You can do it. It's a very simple sound. Just la la; la la; la la; la la. Alright. Wonderful! You guys can sit down."

"Now, the back left quarter of the room. You are going to stand up and you are going to be li li. So you sing li li; li li; li li; li li. Terrific! Okay. Now you guys can all sit down."

"The front left quarter of the room. You guys are going to be chica boom, chica boom, chica boom, chica boom, chica boom, chica boom, chica boom, chica boom. Alright. So you are doing it very rapidly almost in the eighth notes. Chica boom, chica boom, chica boom, chica boom."

"So now everybody stand up. We are going to begin with our front right quarter. They are going to get our pulse going. March, march, march, march; 1-2-3-4. Very nice and strong. Keep that going throughout the whole song."

"Now the back right quarter, ready? La la, la la, la la, la la. Very nice. Now we are going to add our li li's. Li li, li li, li li, li li. How about this. La la, li li, la la, li li, la la, li li, la la. Can you guys do that? Can you la la's and li li's? Go. La la, li li, la la, li li, la la, li li, la la. Perfect! Keep that going throughout the whole song."

"Alright. And adding our front quarter. Chica boom, chica boom, chica boom, chica boom. Very nice. So now you are putting all those sounds together."

Now, facilitator, we are going to sing a song over it. You can do really any song over it.

• HAPPY BIRTHDAY
• MARY HAD A LITTLE LAMB
• THE WHEELS ON THE BUS
• THE ITSY BITSY SPIDER

You split the room into quarters. You give them each a sound or an activity. You put it all together and it all matches just beautifully. And then you sing a song kind of rapidly over the top of it. And it can be a song that a lot of people know that has that 4/4 rhythm, such as Rudolph, the Red-Nosed Reindeer. It's nice and spunky. These nursery rhymes get everyone giggling.

So that's how you make everyone a family orchestra. The other thing that you could do toward the end is speed everybody up and then they just end up laughing and giggling. The family orchestra is a wonderful musical activity to practice rhythm, create social cohesion and break the ice.

Activity #9

Self-Regulation
WALK WITH ME

DESCRIPTION: Walk with me is an activity we use when young children feel nervous, anxious, worried or angry. They might be reluctant to come into the therapy room or leave their classroom. They may not wish to engage, so you make it fun. All you do is simply reach out towards them and say, "Walk with me."

Now, as you walk, you match their pace and add a little something like on the fourth beat; you clap. So you walk, 2, 3 clap. They look at you like this is strange and you smile and ask if they want to join in. Then you ask them if they wish to be the leader. They can add anything from animal sounds to simple movements. For those of you who play with children, you can easily imagine how much this activity helps rapport and engagement.

This is a really nice activity to move around the defensive brain and engage the thinker to partner in a connected and a collaborative way with a student who might be nervous, sad, unhappy or angry. You can even add patterns of sound to the walking activity.

A variation that can be fun is to add large motor movements to your patterns. You can walk four steps like a lion and then two steps like giraffe. Most of all, you can playfully engage the client or student in this light-hearted activity.

Activity #10

Self-Regulation
SHOULDER BLASTS

DESCRIPTION: Shoulder Blasts is a quick energizing activity to help children become more alert. It is a fun activity you can do frequently before a thinking or learning activity. When the children in the group or class master it, then the children can alternate being the leader, which they really enjoy.

RELATED SKILL SETS YOU MAY WISH TO EXPLORE WITH THE CHILDREN:

- Alerting Attention
- Coordination
- Impulse Control
- Motor Management
- Motor Planning
- Motor Sequencing
- Rhythm

MATERIALS: Comfortable clothing.

READY: "OKAY time to come to attention, that means alert and ready to learn. Let's get into ready position and be prepared to blast-off."

LET'S PLAY:

1. "Like many of our activities, we will do three movements in sets of three; you all are becoming familiar with this, right! So for shoulder blast-offs, we begin with our hands straight down at our sides, we lift or shrug our shoulders up then down three times. Okay let's try that, 1-2-3. Great job!"

2. "Now for move #2, we shoot our hands straight up to the sky like rockets directly above our heads. Ready? Up-down-up-down-up-down. Excellent!"

3. "For move #3, we squat down to touch the ground then pop straight up reaching our hands to the sky. Now we are rockets, blasting off. This is great! Let's go for it, squat down and pop up three times. Ready, go!"

4. "Now, can we put them all together? First we'll shrug our shoulders three times, then we'll reach for the sky three times, then we'll squat down and pop up like a rocket three times. The key is we all do it together like a team in training, so we need our rhythm remember, 1-2-3."

5. "Alright, let's do it!"

REVIEW:

1. So how did we do?
2. Was staying together as a group easy or difficult?
3. What did you do to stay with the other kids?
4. Did you watch others?
5. Did you have to slow yourself down or speed yourself up?

Great Work Kids, We Are Getting Better Every Time.

Activity #11

Self-Regulation
GET SEATED

DESCRIPTION: Research shows us that just standing up for 10 seconds increases blood flow to the brain, improving oxygenation and, therefore, cognitive alertness. We can bring our bodies and brains to a state of better attention when we sit then stand and use the large muscles of our legs to further oxygenate our bodies. It takes only about 30 seconds overall, and it's likely you will be smiling by the end.

RELATED SKILL SETS YOU MAY WISH TO EXPLORE WITH THE CHILDREN:

- Balance
- Coordination
- Impulse Control
- Motor Management
- Motor Planning
- Motor Sequencing
- Rhythm

MATERIALS: Comfortable clothing.

READY: Let's stand in ready position with your feet shoulder width apart facing forward.

LET'S PLAY: "Now we are going to reach our hands straight forward and pretend to sit down. You will bend your knees and squat down until your thighs are parallel to the floor. We breathe in as we sit and breathe out as we stand up back to ready position. We pretend to sit down 15 times in a row in rapid succession. Make sure you breathe, because this is tiring. Smile every time you stand up, so you keep your energy up as you use your leg muscles to propel you up and down."

REVIEW:

1. So how did we do?
2. Do you need a minute to catch your breath?
3. If we did this one time every day, do you think our legs would get stronger?
4. Did you throw your arms out in front of you each time you sat down?
5. Did your arm movement make it easier for you to balance?
6. Was that activity easy or difficult?
7. What would you change or add to this activity to keep it interesting?

"Great work! We are getting stronger every day."

Great Work!
We Are Getting Stronger Every Day.

Self-Regulation
JUMP LUNGES

DESCRIPTION: Jump Lunges are an alerting activity that entails thinking, planning and coordination of movement. It's fun to see the children get better as you incorporate this activity into your movement breaks throughout the day.

RELATED SKILL SETS YOU MAY WISH TO EXPLORE WITH THE CHILDREN:

- Balance
- Coordination
- Impulse Control
- Motor Management

- Motor Planning
- Motor Sequencing
- Rhythm

MATERIALS: Comfortable clothing.

READY: "It's fun to jump up in the air and then lunge. As we do this activity, we will feel like athletes warming up for the Olympics. Let's get into ready position because we are going to soar!"

LET'S PLAY: "Jump lunges are an activity we try to do at the same time. Part of the fun is trying to be in unison with our classmates. If we move together all at the same time, we will be moving in synchrony. So this means that some of us will have to jump higher or lunge lower so that we get our timing just right. As you do your jump lunges, keep an eye on your friends so that we try hard to move as a group, almost like a flock of birds all together at the same time."

1. "So let's all stand tall in ready position, but this time we will put our feet together."
2. "Put your arms at your sides."
3. "Now when I say '3' we all jump straight up and when we land we do a lunge with our right leg back and our front knee bent."
4. "Then we jump up from that position and put our left leg back, and our right knee bent. We will do the jump lunges 10 times total, then we will jump back to ready position."
5. "Let's have a lot of energy and really try to jump together. In order to help us keep the rhythm, we will count the lunges out loud together."

REVIEW:

1. So how did we do?
2. Did we all stay together?
3. Did jump lunges wake you up?
4. What was difficult about this activity?
5. What would you change about this activity next time?

Activity #13

Self-Regulation
FOUR CORNERS

DESCRIPTION: Four Corners is a movement-based game that gives students a chance to move, stretch and take a mental break from concentrating on school work. They also have an opportunity to reflect on whether they feel energized or nervous when they play a "wait and see" kind of game.

RELATED SKILL SETS YOU MAY WISH TO EXPLORE WITH THE CHILDREN:

- Balance
- Coordination
- Impulse Control
- Motor Management
- Motor Planning
- Motor Sequencing
- Rhythm

READY: Tell the children you are going to play a game that encourages them to think about how we "stop" and how we "go."

LET'S PLAY: Number each corner of the room 1–4. Draw straws to choose one child to be "It." He or she closes eyes and counts backwards from 10 to 0. While (s)he is counting, the other children must tiptoe around the room until they choose a corner to stand in. When the counter gets to zero, (s)he must call out a number of a corner before opening eyes. The children in that corner must sit back down at their seats. A new "It" is chosen and play continues. The children need to inhibit their impulses to run, change their minds after selecting a corner and open their eyes while being "It." This game encourages alertness, attention to detail and remaining calm.

REVIEW:

1. What did you like about this game?

2. How did you feel?

3. Did you want to change corners?

4. Was it hard to wait to see what number our friend called out?

5. When your corner was chosen to sit out, how did you feel?

Self-Regulation
BIG BEN

DESCRIPTION: Balance and rhythm are central components of learning. When a student moves his body slowly through space, he has to use his senses, proprioception, kinesthetic awareness and motor pacing to move efficiently. This activity teaches self-regulation without saying anything about that skill. We simply do it, like we roll balls, pass pretend bean bags and more.

RELATED SKILL SETS YOU MAY WISH TO EXPLORE WITH THE CHILDREN:

- Balance
- Coordination
- Impulse Control
- Motor Management
- Motor Planning
- Motor Sequencing
- Rhythm

MATERIALS: Comfortable clothing.

READY: "Have you all see those super big clocks, like Big Ben in London? They have hour hands and minute hands, right? Well, we are going to move our legs one at a time with the precision of an enormous clock. We need to move slowly and stay in control, or we will disrupt the time around the world." "Let's get into ready position."

LET'S PLAY: "I am going to name a time of day. We will then swing our left legs straight out to the left at a 45-degree angle like the big hand of a clock, moving with the hour number. We will then pause one second and switch legs and swing our right leg out to the right 45 degrees like the second hand of the clock."

"Our goal is to move as one unit, so we need to keep an eye on our friends and move at the same pace. We will use our Musical Thinking for this one and move our left leg in half notes and our right leg in quarter notes. We'll move the number of minutes or seconds counting aloud with precision together."

Then the teacher or clinician names a time of day such as 11:10 am or 4:25 pm and tells the class when to BEGIN! This activity requires thinking, pacing and inhibition, so have fun with it, it's not a military exercise, it's a motor movement activity. If you wish, you can soon choose one of the group members or classmates to name the time. You can even vary this activity up by having partners face one another and mirror movements, or even have the entire class or group face one another in a circle. Be creative and switch it up.

REVIEW:

1. So how did we do?

2. What was easy about this activity?

3. What was difficult about this activity?

4. Was it easier to be the hour hand or the minute hand?

5. Was it easy or difficult to keep the pace and timing as a group?

6. How could we switch this activity up?

7. What variations could we do next time?

Activity #15

Self-Regulation
VOLCANO

DESCRIPTION: Our interest in music and our participating in song goes back tens of thousands of years. There are some researchers who observe that participating in song was one of the initial ways that human beings began to socialize and connect with one another in order to feel safe. This activity is a song called Volcano that's written to help children become more aware of their calming skills. Ask the children to sit down in their seats, whether it's in your office, on the playground or in the classroom, and tell them that you are going to teach them a song that will help them manage their feelings. It's about a volcano.

LET'S PLAY: "Alright kids, we are going to do a song together called Volcano. It's a song that I made up with my children when they were very young. My hope is that, by the time we learn the song, you guys are able to write and teach a class, or the group, your own song."

Here is how it goes:

"Volcano, volcano I'm going to pop my top.
Volcano, volcano won't you help me stop.
Use my calming skills, help me take deep breaths
Volcano, volcano I'm not going to pop."

REVIEW:

1. Do you ever feel like a volcano?
2. Do you ever feel like you could pop?
3. What do you do not to pop?
4. What are your own personal calming skills?
5. Can you name two calming skills you use so that you don't pop?
6. If you know somebody who is always popping in your life, what kind of song would you write for them?
7. How would you teach them the song; would you use just words, would you use music, would you use movements?
8. If you were going to write your own song about managing your feelings and choosing not to pop, what would those words be?
9. Write them down.
10. Add them to music.

Self-Regulation
RHYTHM BALL

DESCRIPTION: Helping children establish their rhythm and timing often begins with teaching the children how to bounce the playground ball directly in front of themselves on their own. There are two ways to do this: as the facilitator, you can stand across from the child or next to them giving verbal instructions and reinforcing their behavior with specific compliments regarding how they are holding the ball, how consistently they are pushing the ball and how well they are hitting the spot that is designated directly in front of them. It may work best if you bounce a ball at the same time as the student, while standing directly across from them or next to them. This will activate the brain and body's desire to entrain or synchronize, thus helping the child establish a clear beat.

You might also use some of the cuing from Musical Thinking, asking questions such as "Shall we try it in Slow-Mo?" "What will the ball sound like if we bounce in Slow-Mo?" "Are we ready to try some Quick Rick?" Always remember to authentically compliment the child when appropriate.

RELATED SKILL SETS YOU MAY WISH TO EXPLORE WITH THE CHILDREN:

- Balance
- Coordination
- Impulse Control
- Motor Management
- Motor Planning

- Motor Sequencing
- Rhythm
- Sequencing
- Successive Processing

MATERIALS: One 8.5-inch playground ball.

READY: Tell the child that you are going to learn how to bounce a ball. Put a big X or polyspot about 6 inches directly in front of their feet so they are bouncing the ball from waist height directly down to the ground. Ask them stand in ready position and hand them the ball.

"Now we are going to bounce the ball. You are going to hold the ball evenly on each side of the ball and you are going to push the ball or bounce the ball directly in front of you on the designated spot. You are going to try to do this with a consistent pace that sounds like 1 + 2 + 3 + 4 +." As we discussed earlier, the numbers are said on the downbeat, the "and" is said as the child catches the ball. The "and" will drop away as the child gets the hang of it and needs less cuing.

LET'S PLAY: "Okay, give it a try. Push that ball down, very nice, relax your shoulders, bend your knees a little bit and push the ball onto the X." Encourage the children to bounce the ball until they have a consistent rhythm, complimenting them for their rate, speed and effort; you want to see them bouncing the ball in a consistent rhythm. Model the bouncing as needed. Generally, we find that children feel less self-conscious when we are bouncing a ball along with them.

REVIEW:

1. How did you enjoy bouncing the ball?

2. What was easy about bouncing a ball?

3. What was difficult about bouncing the ball?

4. Would you like to bounce the ball between us?

5. Pretend you are the teacher and show me how to bounce the ball.

Activity #17

Self-Regulation
FLIP 'N PUSH

DESCRIPTION: Teaching children how to bounce balls is a wonderful way to help them establish timing and sequencing. We have bounced balls with hundreds of children, many times, and find they do not know how to efficiently bounce the ball, so we teach them how to "Flip 'n Push."

MATERIALS: One racquetball.

RELATED SKILL SETS YOU MAY WISH TO EXPLORE WITH THE CHILDREN:

- Balance
- Coordination
- Impulse Control
- Motor Management
- Motor Planning
- Motor Sequencing
- Rhythm
- Sequencing
- Successive Processing

GET READY: Show the child how to stand with both feet firmly planted shoulder width apart, with toes facing forward, as if one is standing on a line.

LET'S PLAY: Hand the racquetball to the child and tell him we are going to practice how to bounce a ball. Holding the ball in a supine position, rotate the wrist over and push the ball to the ground. "See, I take the ball, flip it and push it." Now the child can imitate you with his own ball.

The child bounces the ball with his right hand eight times and transfers the ball to his left hand and bounces the ball with the same supine then rotating wrist technique. It's helpful to count the beats with the child to cue consistent rhythm.

REVIEW:

1. How did it feel to push the ball instead of throwing it?
2. How did it feel to have such good quality control over pushing the ball?
3. Which hand do you prefer to push the ball with?
4. Was it enjoyable to bounce the ball eight times on each side?
5. If you were teaching another child how to bounce the ball, how would you do it?

Teaching how to bounce a ball using the flip and push technique enhances a child's self-esteem and confidence because many children are expected to pass and throw balls, but are never really taught how to do so. Once you teach a child how to flip and push the ball, they are ready to throw and pass the ball in gym class, at the park and with friends.

Activity #18

Self-Regulation
BOUNCING FOR TWO

DESCRIPTION: Once the child has had the experience of bouncing a playground ball in front of himself, now he is ready to bounce the ball to a partner. Helping children to establish rhythmic bouncing is a foundational step toward self-regulation. Self-regulation is all about energy management, and when children can bounce with a consistent rhythm they can learn how to regulate in other activities such as consistent breathing, yoga movements, Tai Chi and more.

MATERIALS: One 8.5-inch playground ball.

RELATED SKILL SETS YOU MAY WISH TO EXPLORE WITH THE CHILDREN:

- Balance
- Coordination
- Impulse Control
- Motor Management
- Motor Planning
- Motor Sequencing
- Rhythm
- Sequencing
- Successive Processing

READY: Ask the child to get into ready position with toes forward facing the facilitator. Tell the child you are going to bounce the ball between the two of you. Show the child how to hold the ball with their left and right hands evenly on each side of the ball.

LET'S PLAY: "We are going to bounce the ball between ourselves. You can begin by bouncing the ball to me and we are going to try to make a V in between us. So, if you push the ball with both hands into the center spot between us, I will catch it and I will bounce it back. We are going to try to establish a consistent rhythm as we bounce the ball in a V between us, ready? Okay, let's go and let's count as we do it. One, two, three, four. That's perfect. So every time the ball leaves our hands, we are going to say a number, one, two, three, four. That's perfect. Now, as you push the ball, you are pushing it just above your waist into the center spot, then I am catching it above my waist and I am pushing the ball back to you; that's terrific."

REVIEW:

1. Did you enjoy bouncing the ball?
2. What was easy about bouncing the ball?
3. What was difficult about bouncing the ball?
4. If you are going to teach somebody else how to bounce this ball, what instructions would you give them?
5. What would you show them to do?

Activity
#19

Self-Regulation
THE ROCKING V

DESCRIPTION: There are many of ways children can learn how to bounce balls. What we have observed with children is that they develop a preference for a certain size of ball, as well as a specific type of bouncing. Some children like to bounce the racquetball with one hand or from one hand to the other. Other children prefer the playground ball. Ball bouncing is both alerting and calming as it activates the body's natural inclination for rhythm. We have had children bring balls with them to restaurants to help them remain calm while waiting. We have had entire classes bounce balls before a test to alert their brains. We have also used balls in individual therapy, social skill work or executive function training for 5–8 minutes before we do our learning modules. The Rocking V is a calming activity that children like to do when they are anxious or have BIG feelings. It's a natural way to self-modulate.

MATERIALS: A racquetball.

RELATED SKILL SETS YOU MAY WISH TO EXPLORE WITH THE CHILDREN:

- Balance
- Coordination
- Impulse Control
- Motor Management
- Motor Planning
- Motor Sequencing
- Rhythm
- Sequencing
- Successive Processing

READY: Tell the child to stand in ready position because you are going to bounce the ball in a new way. Tell them they are going to take the ball in their left hand and then bounce the ball in a V in front of them to their right hand.

LET'S PLAY: "Alright, this is going to be fun. You are now going to take the ball in your left hand; you are going to bounce it in the center spot and then catch with your right hand and push the ball back and forth between your hands in V."

"So the hard part here is actually keeping your rhythm and timing pushing the ball consistently, catching it with the palm of your hand, then pushing it back. So you can do the flip and push if you'd like. We can also count initially if you'd like a cuing sound to help stay on the beat."

"Do you want to give it a try? Alright here you go, push the ball into the center V, there you go, on the spot and catching it with your other hand, beautiful." "We can use what we learning in Musical Thinking to slow down or speed up our pace. We can even do ball bouncing compositions once we get the hang of it."

REVIEW:

1. Which did you enjoy better, pushing the ball in front of you with two hands or pushing the ball from one hand to the other hand in a V?

2. Did your body want to rock back and forth as you bounced the ball?

3. Was it hard to just stand still and bounce the ball?

4. Do you think you would be more comfortable if you were rocking back and forth a little bit as you pushed the ball?

5. What was difficult about the activity?

6. What was easy about the activity?

7. If you are going to teach somebody else how to do that activity, what instructions and actions would you show them so they could learn?

8. Do you want to be a teacher?

9. Could you could teach me how to bounce the ball in a lateral V?

Activity #20

Self-Regulation
PRETEND PICKLEBALL

DESCRIPTION: Teaching children to be attentive to the social and motor skills of others can be effectively accomplished by playing games. Using their "imaginations" is also a helpful pathway to learning. We play a series of "imaginary" motor games we call Pickleball to show children that you can play any ball game without a ball, simply by using your imagination.

You might have heard of Pickleball: it's basically tennis on a smaller court with a smaller racket and a smaller net. Kids love it. In this series of games, we play pretend Pickleball with just our hands, without a racquet.

RELATED SKILL SETS YOU MAY WISH TO EXPLORE WITH THE CHILDREN:

- Balance
- Coordination
- Imagination
- Impulse Control
- Motor Management
- Motor Planning
- Motor Sequencing
- Rhythm
- Sequencing
- Successive Processing
- Visual Working Memory

MATERIALS: Comfortable clothing.

READY: Ask the child if they've ever played Pickleball. It's like tennis or ping pong, but we can do it in any space, anytime, anywhere, we don't even need a ball, a racket or a net.

Offer to play a version of Pickleball in your office, outside in the parking lot or on the sidewalk or even in your living room. All you need is a space that is about two feet by six feet long.

LET'S PLAY: "We are going to play a game and I'd like you to draw a pretend net. Then we are going to pass a pretend ball over the pretend net. You pass the ball underhand, over the net. I'll let it bounce, pretend to catch it and pretend to pass it back to you. We will do this slowly and with good consistent rhythm. It's kind of like playing tennis without a racket; your hand is the racket and you simply pretend to hold the ball and toss it over the net back and forth. Got it? We are using our imaginations!"

Continue to pass the ball for pretend over the net. You might see lots of giggles, silliness and maybe even a little bit of confusion. But playing pretend is fun, once you get the hang of it. In lesson two, you are going to clarify for the child exactly what this would look like if you were really holding a ball.

REVIEW:

1. What was that experience like for you?

2. What were you thinking?

3. Could you imagine the ball in your hand?

4. Were you tracking the pretend ball with your eyes?

5. What was easy about playing pretend Pickleball?

6. What was difficult about playing pretend Pickleball?

7. If you were going to teach your friend or brother or sister how to play pretend Pickleball, what would you tell them? And what would you show them?

Self-Regulation
PALM PICKLEBALL

DESCRIPTION: You've already completed lesson one of Pretend Pickleball and you did that lesson without a ball. Now in this activity, we add a real ball. There is a body of research that shows us that we can learn using our imaginations. We can also learn by observation, imitation and even motor memory.

RELATED SKILL SETS YOU MAY WISH TO EXPLORE WITH THE CHILDREN:

- Balance
- Coordination
- Impulse Control
- Motor Management
- Motor Planning

- Motor Sequencing
- Rhythm
- Sequencing
- Successive Processing
- Visual Working Memory

MATERIALS: A racquetball.

READY: "So we already played pretend Pickleball without a ball. We drew a net and we passed the pretend ball over the net. Now let's try this game with an actual ball, and see how it feels differently."

LET'S PLAY: Hand the child the racquetball and ask him to draw another pretend net. Tell him "This time, we will pass the real ball over the pretend net. We can count in order to cue our rhythm. I wonder if this will be easier or harder than passing the pretend ball over the net."

Pass the ball back and forth. You may lose it, but that's no problem – go and grab it and do it again. Pass the ball back and forth approximately 20 or 30 times until the child efficiently has solid rhythm, solid timing and is passing the ball competently over the net. This activity is a playful exploration of the difference between using a real object and using a pretend object. Curiously, once the children have passed, thrown or bounced a real ball, they can play pretend ball anywhere anytime.

REVIEW:

1. Did you enjoy this activity?
2. How was it different from playing Pretend Pickleball?
3. Did you find it easier or harder than pretending to play with a ball?
4. Did you find that listening to the sound of the ball was helping you to keep your rhythm and timing?
5. Were you watching the ball as you passed it over the net?
6. What did I look like? Did I look like I was going to catch the ball?
7. If you were going to teach one of your brothers, sisters or friends how to do this activity, what would you say to them and what would you do?

Activity
#22

Self-Regulation
MIRROR PICKLEBALL

DESCRIPTION: Now you've already played Pretend Pickleball without a ball and then Palm Pickleball with a ball. The child has attended to auditory and visual cues. Those memories are stored and, as he plays again with a pretend ball, he might feel like he can see the path of the ball and even hear it bounce, even when the ball is no longer there.

RELATED SKILL SETS YOU MAY WISH TO EXPLORE WITH THE CHILDREN:

- Balance
- Coordination
- Imagination
- Impulse Control
- Motor Management
- Motor Planning

- Motor Sequencing
- Narrative Language
- Rhythm
- Sequencing
- Successive Processing
- Visual Working Memory

READY: "We have now played with a pretend ball and a real ball. We are going to pass the pretend ball over the net one more time and I want us to notice how it feels differently from Palm Pickleball."

LET'S PLAY: "Similar to Pretend Pickleball, in Mirror Pickleball, we will draw our pretend net and pass the ball over the net. Ready, let's give it a go."

You may choose to comment on what seems different. Are you playing more like you have a real ball than the first time? Can the child see or hear the ball, even though it's not there? Now you can talk about the power of visual and auditory memory. You can discuss how memories of motor experiences are stored in our brains. This allows us great flexibility in our learning and play. You might extend this activity by asking the child if he'd like to try pretend Hacky Sack or basketball. We have played entire games of "horse" that feel quite like real basketball with nothing but a pretend ball and our imaginations.

REVIEW:

1. Let's think about Mirror Pickleball: how was it different compared with Pretend Pickleball and Palm Pickleball?
2. Did you feel that, after playing with a real ball, you were able to pretend with more ease?
3. Where can you imagine doing this – can you imagine doing this in the kitchen or outside on the sidewalk or in your backyard?
4. Were you listening for the pretend ball and actually hearing it?
5. What did you see as we passed the pretend ball back and forth over the net?
6. Did you find that you paid better attention once you could imagine holding a real ball?

Activity #23

Self-Regulation
PING AND PONG

DESCRIPTION: There have been times when we have needed activities to teach rhythm, tempo, timing and self-regulation in small spaces, such as at a desk. Ping and Pong developed out of this need. We have played Ping and Pong in our offices, in classrooms and even in a ballroom one time with one hundred adults who used pretend ping pong balls.

RELATED SKILL SETS YOU MAY WISH TO EXPLORE WITH THE CHILDREN:

- Alerting Attention
- Coordination
- Inhibition
- Impulse Control
- Motor Management
- Motor Planning
- Motor Sequencing

- Narrative Language
- Rhythm
- Sequencing
- Successive Processing
- Sustained Attention
- Visual Tracking
- Visual Working Memory

MATERIALS: One ping pong ball for each child.

READY: "We are going to play Ping and Pong now. It's a fun game where we each have a ball and we bounce it on our desks." If you do this as a class, designate one child as A and the other as B, so that you can encourage group synchrony. When you play this several times and the students get the hang of working together in time, they are amazed, confident and so excited by their accomplishment. Feel free to let the children work in groups as well, like a table of four children at a time, two kids on each side. Variations in this activity come naturally and the children love the creativity and leadership opportunity.

LET'S PLAY: "Alright, stand on opposite sides of the desk facing your partner. One of you will begin: you will bounce your ball in a specific rhythm a set number of times, then your partner will bounce his ball in the same rhythm for exactly as many times as you bounced your ball. We will start out with a simple four count and then make it more complicated as we go. Eventually, you will take turns creating compositions or patterns and your partner will imitate you. The key here is to bounce the ping pong ball consistently, just like your partner did. So we need to pay close attention. We are going to drop the balls; they will roll away. No worries, just quietly go pick them up and begin again."

Use Musical Thinking to vary your speed, counts, rhythms and combinations. You can begin with 1-2-3-4, then the other person repeats. You can count or cue to help the children as well, at least initially.

Variations include (but are not limited to):

1-2-3-4 ¦ 1-2-3-4 (Slow Mo)

1-2-3-4 ¦ 1-2-3-4 (Quick Rick)

1-2 *Pause* 3-4 ¦ 1-2 *Pause* 3-4 (Slow Mo)

1-2 *Pause* 3-4 ¦ 1-2 *Pause* 3-4 (Quick Rick)

1-2-3 1-2-3 ¦ 1-2-3 1-2-3

1-2 *Pause* 1-2-3 ¦ 1-2 *Pause* 1-2-3

REVIEW:

1. How did we do?

2. Were we able to stay together as a group?

3. Were you able to follow your partner?

4. Were you in time?

5. What rhythm compositions did you create?

Self-Regulation
I CLAP, YOU CLAP

DESCRIPTION: I Clap, You Clap is a variation on Ping and Pong. Simply use your hands in a clapping motion to create patterns and compositions for your client, student, group or class to do together. Provide opportunities for the children to make up their own patterns, so that every child has an opportunity to be the group leader. You can vary the clapping by adding other sounds as well like taps or snaps. This is a great activity to create a group orchestra, as we have discussed earlier in this book. I Clap, You Clap is a great activity to re-alert your group or class, get everyone working together and create unity among the children.

Section Summary

We hope you have had a wonderful time exploring different aspects of energy management associated with self-regulation. If you have consistently incorporated these exercises into your practice or in your classroom, you are likely seeing changes in the mindsets, behavior and learning of the children with whom you work or teach.

In the next chapter, we shall consider using Musical Thinking to teach Math, specifically fact families and factors. But you will see, with ease, that you could be teaching phonics, vocabulary, foreign language, social skills, communication skills and more.

Musical Thinking and Play Math

chapter 6

In our work, we have a little program called Play Math. It's a neurocognitive motor-based math program we teach to children, schools, clinicians and teachers around the world.

Play Math integrates neuroscience research with occupational therapy, cognitive science, and kinesiology. Play Math is not a curriculum, it's a motor math method founded in the work of Luria, Das, Carpenter, Vygotsky, Fletcher and more. Alternating fine and gross motor movement, play math enhances conceptual math understanding while teaching number composition through play.

"Our goal is simple – to change the trajectory of children's conceptual understanding of fact families (multiplication and division)."

We teach math facts and factors through play using Musical Thinking as a rhythmic tool. Let's apply Musical Thinking to math and see what you think.

In this series of activities, we will teach you the simplest motor movements and math composition strategies. From there, you and your children can make up games, use other sports equipment, draw, play and create.

The Sky is the Limit.

Simple Foundational Play Math Concepts

Play Math is taught in five simple steps.

1. Establish A Rhythmic Beat
2. Mirror Count – Large Ball Bouncing
3. Skip Count – Large Ball Bouncing
4. Slide and Glide – Move the Blocks
5. Repeat The Beat – Large Ball Bouncing

For many children, playing math 15–30 minutes at a time, for 10–20 sessions, is enough for the children to begin to think mathematically. As they begin to succeed, their confidence grows and their imaginations and thinking skills blossom.

Cognitive Tip: Remember we are not teaching, we are playing.

What you will need overall: One playground ball, one tennis or racquetball, one set of Unifix blocks, an 8.5 × 11 inch marker board (the kind that lies flat on a table).

Lets Get
Started.

In this series of activities, we will offer you the words and actions to Play Math with the children whom you care for or with whom you work. I cannot emphasize enough the need to remain playful and child-centered. Although we offer you the words and actions, use your own communication skills and creativity as you play and interact. Play Math can be done 1 on 1, in small groups or in classrooms. It works best when you pair children up together so that they can mentor and help one another. Play Math is a transformative experience for many children. We have helped hundreds of children gain confidence and ignite an interest in math with these empowering activities.

Establishing the Rhythm

Establishing rhythm at the beginning of every Play Math session is central to the Play Math method. There are several Play Math activities designed to help the child develop better motor rhythm. Some children have pretty good rhythm naturally, but often, particularly when a child has difficulty with math, their auditory rhythm and motor rhythm sequencing skills may need support and development.

The first three activities are ways to introduce rhythm to the children. The rhythm activities are scaffolded beginning with a simple ball-passing task, moving to a more complex ball-passing task and ending with a gross motor ball-bouncing task. When we first work with children, we do each activity in order to assess their abilities to maintain a beat and to provide them with choices so that they are empowered to be leaders in Play Math from the outset. You might also have gathered, as you have read through this book, that the activities are flexible and adaptable. Therefore the rhythm activities in Play Math can be used to teach phonics, spelling, vocabulary, foreign languages and more.

Once the children are introduced to establishing the rhythm, you will be ready to Play Math. The child will also be able to choose one of the three rhythm activities as Step 1 of Play Math. First, let's review the three rhythm activities.

Activity
#1

Play Math
PASS TO THE BEAT

DESCRIPTION: Pass to the beat is the first motor activity in Play Math. We simply pass the ball from one hand to another or from one person to another. This exercise is written for two people, but the student or client can practice on their own simply by passing the ball to a beat from one hand to another.

RELATED SKILL SETS YOU MAY WISH TO EXPLORE WITH THE CHILDREN:

- Alerting Attention
- Coordination
- Emotional Regulation
- Focused Attention
- Impulse Control
- Motor Planning

- Motor Sequencing
- Rhythm
- Sequencing
- Successive Processing
- Timing

MATERIALS: One small ball, such as a tennis ball or racquetball.

READY: "We're going to pass the ball now, so let's get ready. We stand directly across from one another, arm's-length apart. We can stretch out our arms in front of ourselves and make sure our hands can touch, then we will know we are the proper distance to pass the ball. Let's try that."

LET'S PLAY: "Now we can pass the ball; I will hold the ball in my left hand and pass it to your right hand." "Now, you can pass it back to me." "Alright, so we want to pass the ball with a consistent rhythm; we will pass it 1-2; 3-4."

If the children have learned "Musical Thinking" you can tell them that you are passing the ball "in half notes" or to the "slow beat."

REVIEW: In Pass to the Beat, we want children to begin the fundamental skill of passing a ball to a beat. That beat or pace is in half notes, approximately 50 beats per minute. Once they are able to pass the ball slowly and consistently to the beat at the 'Slow' rate you can increase the beat to the "Quick" rate, which is quarter notes. As you know, the quarter note in *70 Play Activities* is 85 beats per minute.

Practice passing the ball back and forth in quarter notes. If the child has difficulty maintaining the beat each time you place the ball in the child's hand and they pass it back, support their movements with verbal cuing, in this case counting, 1-2-3-4; 1-2-3-4. You may also use a metronome to establish the beat. When the child is able to pass to the beat, you may move onto activity #2.

Activity #2

Play Math
PASS TO THE BEAT - SQUARE

DESCRIPTION: We have established rhythm and beat via Pass to the Beat, passing the ball back and forth with one hand. Now we extend the children's ability to pass to the beat by teaching them how to hand the ball off in a square.

RELATED SKILL SETS YOU MAY WISH TO EXPLORE WITH THE CHILDREN:

- Alerting Attention
- Coordination
- Emotional Regulation
- Focused Attention
- Inhibition
- Impulse Control
- Motor Planning
- Motor Sequencing
- Rhythm
- Sequencing
- Successive Processing
- Sustained Attention
- Timing

MATERIALS: One small ball, such as a tennis ball or racquetball.

READY: "We're going to pass the ball in a square now, so let's get ready. We stand directly across from one another, arm's-length apart. We can stretch out our arms in front of ourselves and make sure our hands can touch, then we will know we are the proper distance to pass the ball. Let's try that."

LET'S PLAY: "Now we can pass the ball, I will hold the ball in my left hand and pass it to your right hand, then you will pass it to your left hand, then you will pass it to my right hand. I will then do the same passing the ball back to you." "The counts go, 1 to you, 2 from your right to your left, 3 from your left to my right, 4 from my right to my left." "Our beat is in half notes, we could count 1 and 2 and 3 and 4 and." "Let's try this four times."

REVIEW: Pass to the Beat – Square is a bit more complex. If the child does not get it easily, use a metronome or count the beats out with the child. It's important for the child to count with you. The more active the child is in this activity, the faster he will get the beat. If you are in a group or class, you can have the children work with partners.

Now that the child understands what the beats feel like, they are ready to move on to bouncing the playground size ball.

Activity #3

Play Math
BOUNCE TO THE BEAT - BIG BALL BOUNCE

DESCRIPTION: The child has now had the experience of passing the ball to a beat. We scaffold up to a slightly more difficult action bouncing a ball instead of passing it. Bouncing the ball takes a bit better timing, it is also a gross motor movement, so more of the body is working together.

If you wish, you can take blue painter's tape and make a big X, approximately 8–12 inches big, if you feel a target will help your child or student manage his space better. Some children have difficulty imagining a line between you, a plane in which they bounce the ball. The X can be a nice visual cue to start. Over time, you will no longer need the X.

RELATED SKILL SETS YOU MAY WISH TO EXPLORE WITH THE CHILDREN:

- Alerting Attention
- Coordination
- Emotional Regulation
- Focused Attention
- Inhibition
- Impulse Control
- Motor Planning
- Motor Sequencing
- Rhythm
- Sequencing
- Successive Processing
- Sustained Attention
- Timing

MATERIALS: One playground ball.

READY: "You've done such a great job! We're going to bounce the big ball now. We'll stand in ready position across from one another with our feet facing forward. I'll bounce the ball to you and you bounce it back." "I've put a big X on the floor, we'll aim for the X as we bounce the ball back and forth." Finding the proper distance between you and the student may come naturally; if it doesn't, try a width of about 4 feet and lengthen or shorten the space depending on the needs and abilities of the student.

LET'S PLAY: "There is a spot between us, see it, marked with an X? We're going to bounce the ball to one another, almost in a V, hitting the X right in the middle. The X is there to help us keep up a good consistent rhythm. We bounce the ball in half notes at first counting 1 and 2 and 3 and 4 and. Let's give it a try."

"That's great. Now we are ready to count as we bounce. So we imagine we are actually pushing the ball toward the X and we count as we push. Let's try that."

"In order to get ready to practice our numbers, let's alternate counting as we push the ball, so I'll say 1 and you say 2 and so on."

The student and the teacher now bounce the ball to one another counting by ones. Then the teacher encourages the student to be the mentor. We have found over and over again that when the children are the leaders, they learn faster and are more invested in the activities.

"One more thing, it's more fun when you are the leader. So now you will start the counting and I will follow you; we'll alternate 1, 2, 3, 4. Let's try it for two measures, so we'll count 1–4 two times. Ready, you're the leader, you start."

"Good work, we're ready to add some math."

REVIEW: Reflect on the child's ability to establish a smooth consistent rhythm. Was the child able to bounce the ball straight, making a V between the two of you? Did the child count as he bounced the ball?

You now have three variations of activities to help the children with whom you work or play establish clear consistent rhythm. You will have the ability to ask the child or children with whom you are playing math, how they'd like to establish the rhythm before each Play Math session. Most children will choose a preferred method and then you will mirror count and skip count using that activity, be it with Pass to the Beat or Bounce to the Beat.

Next Step: Mirror Counting

Fundamentally, rhythm is at the core of Play Math. I have seen with hundreds of children, specifically those with learning challenges, who often cannot keep a consistent yet simple beat. Because rhythm is central to entrainment, a biologically-based skill necessary for the learning of language, we integrated rhythm with fine and gross motor movement with astonishing results. Auditory-motor entrainment, the ability to align motor actions with an external auditory beat, is a crucial component of learning. So we bounce, tap and even drum, establishing automaticity of rhythmic movement as a core feature of Play Math.

In this next section, we will explore how we alternate the large motor ball bouncing (or passing racquetballs, if the student prefers) with moving small blocks to learn counting and math factors.

Each time we Play Math with a child, we will do five simple steps, overall. The consistency of these steps is important because the child develops mastery over the method, and this increases participation, confidence and learning.

1. We will establish the rhythm.

2. Once we have a nice solid rhythm, we will ask the child if he wishes to mirror count a number with us.

3. Next we will skip count that number.

4. When we get stuck or have difficulty knowing which number is next, we will sit down and move blocks from left to right to "see" the numbers.

5. Last we will "Repeat the Beat." Once we have learned a few more numbers in the skip counting sequence, we will stand up again and skip count. Each time we move from the ball bouncing to the block moving, the child will have an opportunity to fire more neurons, thus encouraging memory encoding and storage.

There are many times we will "play" with a specific number for several days in a row. We wait until the child has mastered skip counting each fact family forward (as an example, 3's: 3-6-9-12-15-18-21-24-27-30) before we move on to another number. When the children become more proficient at skip counting using the blocks and balls, we might even bounce fact families backwards. We might play with the blocks and look at how numbers fit together. It's an organic process; we move with the child. If the child observes a relationship between 3 and 6, perhaps stating that two 3's make a 6, we might stack the blocks and see how they fit together. We can place two 3's on a 6 and see that two 3's make a 6. Children adore observing the number relationships; it makes meaningful sense of math facts and factors.

We take our time. We play. We have fun. We do not rush. We know the brain will respond to the cognitive and motor activities by firing more neurons and creating better "highways" for memory, so we trust the process and take our time.

Now we are ready for a bit of
mirror counting.

Activity #4

Play Math
MIRROR COUNTING

DESCRIPTION: Although you may be used to mirror counting or skip counting beginning with 2's, in Play Math, we begin with 10, then 5. Why? Because most children learn how to skip count 10's and 5's in the course of their daily lives before they learn 2's. Many five-year-olds can skip count 10's with ease; they have often come across this activity in their lives or with their families before they ever get to school. Cognitively speaking, the order of skip counting the brain understands with the most ease is 10, 5, 2, 3, 4, 6, 7, 8, 9.

The teacher or clinician introduces mirror counting once the rhythm has been established. The examples I provide you here will be with 10's. You can then generalize the sentences and actions to 5, 2, 3, 4, 6, 7, 8, and 9.

RELATED SKILL SETS YOU MAY WISH TO EXPLORE WITH THE CHILDREN:

- Alerting Attention
- Coordination
- Emotional Regulation
- Focused Attention
- Inhibition
- Impulse Control
- Motor Planning
- Motor Sequencing
- Rhythm
- Sequencing
- Successive Processing
- Sustained Attention
- Timing

MATERIALS: One playground ball.

READY: "We really have the beat down. It sounds great. Let's add some numbers. When I push the ball, I'll say a number. When you push it back, you repeat the number I said. We will bounce the ball and say our numbers with a nice strong beat." Although we write "bounce" the ball in a V between you in this section, remember, you can let the child choose to pass, pass in a square or bounce the ball. This helps you match the needs, interests and motivation of each student with the Play Math method. Personalizing activities and providing children options empowers them and gives them confidence.

LET'S PLAY: "Ready, 10 (10) 20 (20) 30 (30) 40 (40) 50 (50) 60 (60) 70 (70) 80 (80) 90 (90) 100 (100)." "Great job! Pretty soon you'll be teaching me!"

Bounce the ball between you and the child creating a nice V between you with the ball. As you bounce the ball say 10, then 20, then 30 and so on to 100. Remember, the number is said on the beat. If you start the number as the ball leaves your hands, that timing is usually easy to catch on to and pleasing to the brain.

There may be moments when you lose the ball. Have fun when you chase after it. This is to be relaxed and engaging. Next, you'll skip count 10's and then it's time to open the blocks. Remember, anytime you get "stuck" simply move to the base ten blocks and "slide and glide" to see and count the numbers.

Activity #5

Play Math
SKIP COUNTING

DESCRIPTION: When the child is proficient at mirror counting 10's with you, you can start the next step, which is to skip count 10s. See, super simple, eh?

RELATED SKILL SETS YOU MAY WISH TO EXPLORE WITH THE CHILDREN:

- Alerting Attention
- Coordination
- Emotional Regulation
- Focused Attention
- Inhibition
- Impulse Control
- Motor Planning

- Motor Sequencing
- Rhythm
- Sequencing
- Successive Processing
- Sustained Attention
- Timing

MATERIALS: One playground ball.

READY: "We did that so well, shall we try to alternate the numbers? I say 10, you say 20 and so on? I think we can do it. Great job! Now let's build some blocks and see what 10's look like."

LET'S PLAY: Bounce the ball between you and the child with a nice constant rhythm. As you bounce the ball say 10, then 20, then 30 and so on to 100. Smile a lot! Have Fun! When the child appears confident, you can hand him the ball and let him be the leader. Once you have reached 100, you can move to the blocks to reinforce the learning with fine motor movement, tactile memory and visualization. Let's review Slide and Glide, so it's an easy transition for you all.

Activity #6

Play Math
SLIDE AND GLIDE

DESCRIPTION: In Play Math, we alternate bouncing the ball and skip counting with sliding and gliding base ten blocks on a marker board. You can imagine that you are bouncing the ball in close proximity to a table with two chairs or a flat surface; the floor will even do. I have Played Math with children on playgrounds, behind schools and even in a swimming pool.

You will have some base ten blocks available to the child for this activity. Having tried many base ten blocks, I have observed that the children like Unifix Cubes best. Traditional base ten blocks are all attached. You get bars of 2's, 3's, 4's, etc. If you have these blocks, you can surely use them. I'd also suggest you try Unifix Cubes or Learning Cubes.

Unifix Cubes come as individual units. So, if we are sliding and gliding 10's, as an example, we need to "build the numbers." The time spent building 10–20 bars of 10's (or whatever number you are working on) in cognitive science might be considered "consolidation time" – a time for the brain to take a pause, rest and store what it has been practicing and learning. This pause in the action is beneficial to the teacher/clinician: student/client relationship as well, because it provides a moment to rest, chat and work together to make something you will be using in that Play Math session.

RELATED SKILL SETS YOU MAY WISH TO EXPLORE WITH THE CHILDREN:

- Alerting Attention
- Coordination
- Emotional Regulation
- Focused Attention
- Inhibition
- Impulse Control
- Motor Planning

- Motor Sequencing
- Rhythm
- Sequencing
- Successive Processing
- Sustained Attention
- Timing

MATERIALS: Unifix Cubes or small single unit blocks.

READY: To play Slide and Glide, you sit down at the table or on the floor with the child or children and they build the bars of numbers they will be gliding. Let's consider 10's, since that is what we mirror and skip counted.

LET'S PLAY: The teacher says, "Let's build 10's and see what they look like. Here are some blocks; put them together so we have 10 bars of 10 units." "Here, I'll help." You all build bars of 10, then you place them on the left-hand side of the marker board. You can place a few bars or all of them, depending on how well the child knows 10's.

"See, each bar is 10 individual units, so each bar is a 10. Now we simply slide one bar to the right at a time, counting 10's as we go. Here, you slide them and we can count together. 10, 20, 30, 40, 50, 60, 70, 80, 90, 100! That was great! 10's are just the start; wait until we are counting 6's, 7's, 8's and 9's, you'll know your math facts forward and backward."

If a child gets stuck and does not know the next number, the child can always use his index finger to count the individual blocks. We encourage touching and counting the blocks, as this multi-sensory activity fires different neurons than are fired just using the visual centers of the brain. We also try to move the children from counting on their fingers to actually touching the blocks because this aids in their ability to "image" (see) the blocks in their minds as they move to mental math.

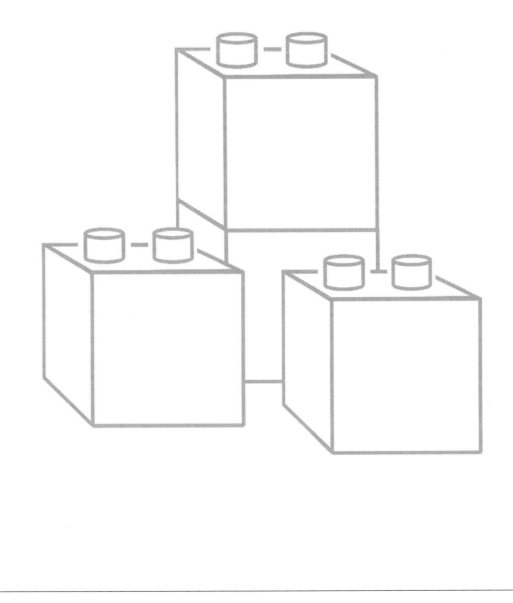

Activity #7

Play Math
REPEAT THE BEAT

DESCRIPTION: The child has now had the experience of skip counting, mirror counting and sliding and gliding the numbers. Now it's time to enhance the automaticity of their learning by bouncing the playground ball once again, this time to quarter notes, as they are retrieving what they have learned.

Going back to activity #5, you will stand across from the child and bounce the playground ball while skip counting the numbers you have learned.

COGNITIVE TIP: Remember, depending on the child, you might have only skip counted or slided and glided to 40 or 50. Wherever you have stopped, repeat the beat to that number. On occasion, particularly with larger numbers, we spend several sessions completing the five-step process, slowly adding a number or two. We do not wish to overload the child's working memory; we want to take the time to allow the child to remember the numbers to enhance memory and automaticity. So take your time, going just a few numbers beyond what the child has learned well.

RELATED SKILL SETS YOU MAY WISH TO EXPLORE WITH THE CHILDREN:

- Alerting Attention
- Coordination
- Emotional Regulation
- Focused Attention
- Inhibition
- Impulse Control
- Motor Planning
- Motor Sequencing
- Rhythm
- Sequencing
- Successive Processing
- Sustained Attention
- Timing

MATERIALS: One playground ball.

READY: "You've done such a great job! We're going to bounce the big ball again to practice the numbers we have learned. We'll stand in ready position across from one another with our feet facing forward. I'll bounce the ball to you and you bounce it back. We will be skip counting the fact family we have been practicing. First let's skip count it forward, then we might have some fun and skip count it backward as well."

LET'S PLAY: "We have been playing with 10's. First, we mirror counted 10's. Then we skip counted 10's. Then we did the slide and glide with 10's. We did that all in half-notes, as we were learning our 10's. Now let's skip count them again while we bounce the ball. When we feel we have them in our memory, we will speed up our bouncing to quarter notes. Let's give it a try. You can be the leader, ready: 10, 20, 30, 40, 50, 60, 70, 80, 90, 100."

Section Summary

Now that you understand the basic five-step method, you can play with 10's, 5's, then 2's, 3's, 4's, 6's, 7's, 8's and 9's. This process may take weeks or months, depending on the child's starting point, as well as their ability to learn and remember. Take your time, be playful, allow the child to teach you, just a few minutes each day. This lays the foundation for all sorts of advanced strategies as the child's conceptual math is becoming automated. You can go on to play games with fact families, you can skip count well-remembered fact families backwards, you can use the blocks to show the child how multiplication and division are opposites and more. The key is that you have used a multi-sensory motor-based strategy to aid the child in experiencing fact families in a new way, and increasing conceptual and creative thinking.

Playing math is a fabulous way to engage children in learning with movement, while reducing anxiety and improving knowledge. Have fun with it, make up games, count backward, and after you do multiplication, use the strategies to do division as well.

In Conclusion

In each of our lives, we have passions, interests, causes or activities that encourage us to get up each day with a desire to make a difference. A primary interest for us is to help children understand how their brains work, so that they experience learning as more empowering and less of a mystery. Over the 30 years that we have played with children, they have taught us more than we have taught them. We express our deep thanks to all the beautiful children with whom we have worked. You might share in this feeling with us. What we have done with *70 Play Activities* is structure, organize and memorialize games created with the children in our offices and schools, so that the activities can be done by children in a wide variety of settings. Be they in a township in South Africa or on an island in the Pacific, most of these activities need little more than love and imagination, so they can be played by all children who wish to grow and learn. We hope you take them, use them, adapt them and share them. Together we can make a difference.

With the **Deepest Gratitude,**
We **Thank You** for Caring for Children.

Best,

Lynne Kenney & Rebecca Comizio

Bibliography

Albert, N. B., Robertson, E. M., & Miall, R. C. (2009). The resting human brain and motor learning. *Current Biology, 19*(12), 1023–1027.

Alexander, A. W., Slinger-Constant, A-M. (2004). Current status of treatments of dyslexia: Critical review. *J Child Neurol., 19*, 744–758.

Anderson, P. (2002). Assessment and development of executive function (EF) during childhood. *Child Neuropsychology, 8*, 71–82.

Barkley, R. (2012). *Executive Functions: What They Are, How They Work, and Why They Evolved*. New York: Guildford Press.

Barros, R. M., Silver, E. J., & Stein, R. E. K. (2009). School recess and group classroom behavior. *Pediatrics, 123*, 431–436.

Bialer, D., & Miller, L. J. (2011). *No Longer A SECRET: Unique Common Sense Strategies for Children with Sensory or Motor Challenges*. Arlington, Texas: Sensory World.

Biel, L., & Peske, N. (2009). *Raising a Sensory Smart Child: The Definitive Handbook for Helping Your Child with Sensory Processing Issues*. London: Penguin Books.

Bodrova, E., & Leong, D. J. (2007). *Tools of the Mind: The Vygotskian Approach to Early Childhood Education*. New York: Merrill/Prentice-Hall.

Brown, Peter C., Roediger, H. L, & McDaniel, M. A. (2014). *Make It Stick: The Science of Successful Learning*. Cambridge, MA: Belknap Press.

Budni, J., Bellettini-Santos, T., Mina, F., Garcez, M. L., & Zugno, A. I. (2015). The involvement of BDNF, NGF and GDNF in aging and Alzheimer's disease. *Aging and Disease, 6*(5), 331–341.

Bushnell, E. W., & Boudreau, J. P. (1993, Aug). Motor development and the mind: The potential role of motor abilities as a determinant of aspects of perceptual development. *Child Development, 64*(4), 1005–1021.

Cameron, C. E., Brock, L. L., Murrah, W. M., Bell, L. H., Worzalla, S. L., Grissmer, D., & Morrison, F. J. (2012). Fine motor skills and executive function both contribute to kindergarten achievement. *Child Development, 83*(4), 1229–1244.

Campbell, D. & Doman, A. (2012). *Healing at the Speed of Sound: How What We Hear Transforms Our Brains and Our Lives*. New York: Hudson Street Press.

Carpenter, T., Franke Loef, M., & Levi, L. (2003). *Thinking Mathematically: Integrating Arithmetic & Algebra in Elementary School*. Portsmouth, NH: Heinemann.

Castelli, D. M., Hillman, C. H., Buck, S. M., & Erwin, H. E. (2007). Physical fitness and academic achievement in third- and fifth-grade students. *Journal of Sport and Exercise Psychology, 29*, 239–252.

Castles, A., & Coltheart, M. (2004). Is there a causal link from phonological awareness to success in learning to read? *Cognition, 91*, 77–111.

Center on The Developing Child: Harvard University. (2015). *Enhancing and Practicing Executive Function Skills with Children from Infancy to Adolescence*. Cambridge, Massachusetts.

Corriveau, K., Pasquini, E., & Goswami, U. (2007). Basic auditory processing skills and specific language impairment: A new look at an old hypothesis. *Journal of Speech Language and Hearing Research, 50*(3), 647–666.

Corriveau K. H., & Goswami, U. (2009). Rhythmic motor entrainment in children with speech and language impairments: Tapping to the beat. *Cortex, 45*, 119–130.

Cumming, R., Wilson, A., Leong, V., Colling, L. J., & Goswami, U. (2015) Awareness of rhythm patterns in speech and music in children with specific language impairments. *Front. Hum. Neurosci., 9*, 672.

Das, J. P., & Naglieri, J. (1994). *Assessment of Cognitive Processes: The PASS Theory of Intelligence*. Boston, MA: Allyn & Bacon.

Davis, C. L., Tomporowski, P. D., McDowell, J. E., Austin, B. P., Miller, P. H., Yanasak, N. E., Allison, J. D., Naglieri, J. A. (2011). Exercise improves executive function and achievement and alters brain activation in overweight children: A randomized controlled trial. *Health Psychology: Official Journal of the Division of Health Psychology, American Psychological Association, 30*(1), 91–98.

Davis, C. L., Tomporowski, P. D., Boyle, C. A., Waller, J. L., Miller, P. H., Naglieri, J. A., & Gregoski, M. (2007). Effects of aerobic exercise on overweight children's cognitive functioning: a randomized controlled trial. *Research Quarterly for Exercise and Sport, 78*(5), 510–519.

Dawson, P. (2009). *Smart but Scattered: The Revolutionary "Executive Skills" Approach to Helping Kids Reach Their Potential*. New York: Guilford Press.

Dawson, P. (2010). *Executive Skills in Children and Adolescents, Second Edition: A Practical Guide to Assessment and Intervention*. New York: Guilford Press.

del Campo, N., Chamberlain, S. R., Sahakian, B. J., Robbins, T. W. (2011). The roles of dopamine and noradrenaline in the pathophysiology and treatment of attention-deficit/hyperactivity disorder. *Biol Psychiatry, 69*(12), e145–5710.

Demers, M. M., McNevin, N., & Azar, N. R. (2013). ADHD and motor control: A review of the motor control deficiencies associated with attention deficit/hyperactivity disorder and current treatment options. *Crit Rev Phys Rehabil Med, 25*, 231–910.

Diamond, A. (2015). Effects of physical exercise on executive functions: Going beyond simply moving to moving with thought. *Annals of Sports Medicine and Research, 2*(1), 1011.

Diamond, A., & Lee, K. (2011). Interventions shown to aid executive function development in children 4–12 years old. *Science, 333*(6045), 959–964.

Diamond, A., Barnett, W. S., Thomas, J., & Munro, S. (2007). Preschool Program Improves Cognitive Control. *Science (New York, N.Y.), 318*(5855), 1387–1388.

Diamond, A. (2000). Close interrelation of motor development and cognitive development and of the cerebellum and prefrontal cortex. *Child Development, 71*, 44–56.

Dishman, R. K., Berthoud, H. R., Booth, F. W., Cotman, C. W., Edgerton, V. R., Fleshner, M. R., … Zigmond, M. J. (2006). Neurobiology of exercise. *Obesity (Silver Spring), 14*, 345–356.

Drollette, E. S., Scudder, M. R., Raine, L. B., Moore, R. D., Saliba, B. J., Pontifex, M. B., et al. (2014). Acute exercise facilitates brain function and cognition in children who need it most: An ERP study of individual differences in inhibitory control capacity. *Dev Cogn Neurosci, 7*, 53–64.

Eaton, H. (2010). *Brain School*. Canada: Glia Press.

Eide, B., & Eide, F. (2012). *The Dyslexic Advantage: Unlocking the Hidden Potential of the Dyslexic Brain*. New York: Hudson Street Press.

Etnier, J. L., Nowell, P. M., Landers, D. M., & Sibley, B. A. (2006). A meta-regression to examine the relationship between aerobic fitness and cognitive performance. *Brain Res Brain Res Rev, 52*(1), 119–130.

Gazzaniga, M. S. Ashbury, C. & Rich, B. (2008). *Learning, Arts, and the Brain: The Dana Consortium Report on Arts and Cognition*. New York: Dana Foundation.

Gordon, R. L., Magne, C. L., & Large, E. W. (2011). EEG Correlates of song prosody: A new look at the relationship between linguistic and musical rhythm. *Frontiers in Psychology, 2*, 352.

Gordon R. L., Fehd, H. M., & McCandliss, B. D. (2015). Does music training enhance literacy skills? A meta-analysis. *Frontiers in Psychology, 6*, 1777.

Goswami, U. (2012a). "Language, music, and children's brains: a rhythmic timing perspective on language and music as cognitive systems," in *Language and Music as Cognitive Systems*, eds P. Rebuschat, M. Rohrmeier, J. A. Hawkings, & I. Cross. Oxford: Oxford University Press, 292–301.

Goswami, U. (2012b). Entraining the brain: applications to language research and links to musical entrainment. *Empir. Musicol. Rev., 7*, 57–63.

Goswami, U., & Leong, L. (2013). Speech rhythm and temporal structure: converging perspectives? *Lab. Phonol., 4*, 67–92.

Griffin, É.W., Mullally, S., Foley, C., Warmington, S. A., O'Mara, S. M., & Kelly, A. M. (2011). Aerobic exercise improves hippocampal function and increases BDNF in the serum of young adult males. *Physiol Behav, 104*, 934–941.

Haskins, E. C. (2012). *Cognitive Rehabilitation Manual: Translating Evidence-Based Recommendations into Practice*. Virginia: ACRM Publishing.

Hausen, M., Torppa, R., Salmela, V. R., Vainio, M., & Särkämö, T. (2013). Music and speech prosody: a common rhythm. *Frontiers in Psychology, 4*, 566.

Haywood, H. C. (2013). What is cognitive education? The view from 30,000 feet. *Journal of Cognitive Education & Psychology, 12*(1).

Health Canada, Canadian Society for Exercise Physiology. (2002). Canada's Physical Activity Guide for Youth. Ottawa: Minister of Public Works and Government Services Canada.

Hill, E. L., Bishop, D., & Nimmo-Smith, L. (1998). Representational gestures in developmental coordination disorder and specific language impairment: Error-types and the reliability of ratings. *Human Movement Science, 17*, 655–678.

Hillman, C. H., Castelli, D. M., Buck, S. M. (2005). Aerobic fitness and neurocognitive function in healthy preadolescent children. *Medicine & Science in Sports & Exercise, 37*(11), 1967–1974.

Hillman, C. H., Erickson, K. I., & Kramer, A. F. (2008). Be smart, exercise your heart: Exercise effects on brain and cognition. *Nature Reviews Neuroscience, 9*, 58–65.

Hillman, C. H., Pontifex, M. B., Raine, L. B., Castelli, D. M., Hall, E. E., & Kramer, A. F. (2009). The effect of acute treadmill walking on cognitive control and academic achievement in preadolescent children. *Neuroscience, 159*(3), 1044–1054.

Hodgson, K., Hutchinson, A. D., & Denson, L. (2014). Nonpharmacological treatments for ADHD: a meta-analytic review. *J Atten Disord, 18*(4), 275–8210.

Ito, Masao. (2011). *The Cerebellum: Brain for an Implicit Self.* London: FT Press.

Janssen, I., & LeBlanc, A. G. (2010). Systematic review of the health benefits of physical activity and fitness in school-aged children and youth. *The International Journal of Behavioral Nutrition and Physical Activity, 7*, 40.

Ma, J. K, Le Mare, L., & Gurd, B. J. (2015). Four minutes of in-class high-intensity interval activity improves selective attention in 9- to 11-year olds. *Applied Physiology, Nutrition, and Metabolism, 40*(3), 238– 244.

Jensen, E. (2005). *Teaching with the Brain in Mind.* Virginia: ASCD.

Kawai, R., Markman, T., Poddar, R., Ko, R., Fantana, A. L., Dhawale, A. K., et al. (2015). Motor cortex is required for learning but not for executing a motor skill. *Neuron*, 1–14.

Kenney, L. (2016). *Musical Thinking: 5 Simple Steps to Teaching Children How They Think.* Scottsdale, AZ: Unhooked Books.

Kenney, L. (2009). *The Family Coach Method.* Pittsburgh: St. Lynn's Press.

Kenney, L. & Young, W. (2015). *Bloom: 50 things to say, think and do with anxious, angry and over-the-top kids.* Scottsdale, AZ: Unhooked Books.

Kenney, (2016). *Bloom Your Room: The Social-Emotional Literacy Art Collection For Classrooms (Ages 4-12)*, Scottsdale, AZ: Move2Think, LLC.

Kovelman, I., Norton, E. S., Christodoulou, J. A., Gaab, N., Lieberman, D. A., Triantafyllou, C., . . . Gabrieli, J. D. E. (2012). Brain basis of phonological awareness for spoken language in children and its disruption in dyslexia. *Cerebral Cortex (New York, NY), 22*(4), 754–764.

Koziol, L. (2014). *The Myth of Executive Functioning: Missing Elements in Conceptualization, Evaluation, and Assessment.* New York: Springer.

Koziol, L. & Budding, D. (2009). *Subcortical Structures and Cognition: Implications for Neuropsychological Assessment.* New York: Springer.

Koziol, L. F., Budding, D., Andreasen, N., D'Arrigo, S., Bulgheroni, S., Imamizu, H., . . . Yamazaki, T. (2014). Consensus paper: The cerebellum's role in movement and cognition. *Cerebellum (London, England), 13*(1), 151–177.

Kraus, N., Slater, J., Thompson, E. C., Hornickel, J., Strait, D. L., Nicol, T., et al. (2014b). Music enrichment programs improve the neural encoding of speech in at-risk children. *J. Neurosci., 34*, 11913–11918.

Lakes, K. D., & Hoyt, W. T. (2004). Promoting self-regulation through school-based martial arts training. *Journal of Applied Developmental Psychology, 25*, 283–302.

Large, E. W., & Jones, M. R. (1999). The dynamics of attending: How people track time-varying events. *Psychological Review, 106*, 119–159.

Lengel, T. L., & Kuczala, M. S. (Eds). (2010). *The Kinesthetic Classroom: Teaching and Learning Through Movement*, California: Corwin.

Leong, V., & Goswami, U. (2014). Assessment of rhythmic entrainment at multiple timescales in dyslexia: Evidence for disruption to syllable timing. *Hear. Res., 308*, 141–161.

Levitan, D. (2007). This Is Your Brain on Music: The Science of a Human Obsession. Plume/Penguin.

Lezak, M. D., Howieson, D. B., & Loring, D. W. (2004). *Neuropsychological Assessment* (4th ed.). New York: Oxford University Press.

Lieberman, M. D. (2013). Social: Why our brains are wired to connect. New York, NY: Crown

Lubans, D. R., Morgan, P. J., Cliff, D. P., Barnett, L. M., & Okely, A. D. (2010). Fundamental movement skills in children and adolescents: Review of associated health benefits. *Sports Medicine*, 40(12), 1019–1035.

Mathai, A., & Smith, Y. (2011). The corticostriatal and corticosubthalamic pathways: Two entries, one target. So what? *Frontiers in Systems Neuroscience, 5*, 64.

McCullough, M. J., Gyorkos, A. M., & Spitsbergen, J. M. (2013). Short-term exercise increases GDNF protein levels in spinal cord of young and old rats. *Neuroscience, 240,* 258–268.

Mehta, R., Ashley Shortz, A., & Benden, M. (2015). Standing up for learning: A pilot investigation on the neurocognitive benefits of stand-biased school desks. *International Journal of Environmental Research and Public Health, 13*(2): 59.

Merrett, D. L., Peretz, I., & Wilson, S. J. (2013). Moderating variables of music training-induced neuroplasticity: A review and discussion. *Front. Psychol., 4,* 606.

Miendlarzewska, E. A., & Trost, W. J. (2013). How musical training affects cognitive development: Rhythm, reward and other modulating variables. *Frontiers in Neuroscience, 7,* 279.

Mullender-Wijnsma, M. J., Hartman, E., de Greeff, J. W., Bosker, R. J., Doolaard, S., & Visscher, C. (2015). Moderate-to-vigorous physically active academic lessons and academic engagement in children with and without a social disadvantage: A within subject experimental design. *BMC Public Health, 15,* 404.

Mullender-Wijnsma, M. J., Hartman, E., de Greeff, J. W., Bosker, R. J., Doolaard, S., & Visscher, C. (2015). Improving academic performance of school-age children by physical activity in the classroom: 1-year program evaluation. *J Sch Health, 85,* 365–371.

Murray, N. G., Low, B. J., Hollis, C., Cross, A. W., & Davis, S. M. (2007). Coordinated school health programs and academic achievement: a systematic review of the literature. *J. Sch. Health, 77*(9), 589–600.

Murray, G. K., Veijola, J., Moilanen, K., Miettunen, J., Glahn, D. C., Cannon, T. D., et al. (2006). Infant motor development is associated with adult cognitive categorisation in a longitudinal birth cohort study. *Journal of Child Psychology and Psychiatry, 47,* 25–29.

Naglieri, J. A., & Johnson, D. (2000). *Effectiveness of a cognitive strategy intervention to improve math calculation based on the PASS theory.* Journal of Learning Disabilities, 33, 591–597.

Overy, K. (2003). Dyslexia and music: from timing deficits to musical intervention. *Ann. N. Y. Acad. Sci., 999,* 497–505.

Patel, A. D. (2010). *Music, Language, and the Brain.* New York, NY: Oxford University Press.

Patel, A. D. (2011). Why would musical training benefit the neural encoding of speech? The OPERA hypothesis. *Front. Psychol., 2,* 142.

Patel, A. D. (2014). Can nonlinguistic musical training change the way the brain processes speech? The expanded OPERA hypothesis. *Hear. Res., 308,* 98–108.

Pérez-Álvarez, F., & Timoneda, C. (2007). A better look at intelligent behavior. Hauppauge, NY: Nova Science Publishers, Inc.

Physical Activity Guidelines for Americans. (2008). U.S. Department of Health and Human Services.

Piek, J. P., Dawson, L., Smith, L. M., & Gasson, N. (2008). The role of early fine and gross motor development on later motor and cognitive ability. *Human Movement Science, 27,* 668–681.

Piek, J. P., Dyck, M. J., Nieman, A., Anderson, M., Hay, D., Smith, L. M. et al. (2004). The relationship between motor coordination, executive functioning, and attention in school aged children. *Archives of Clinical Neuropsychology, 19,* 1063–1076.

Raudsepp, L., & Pall, P. (2006). The relationship between fundamental motor skills and outside school physical activity of elementary school children. *Pediatr Exerc Sci, 18,* 426–435.

Ratey, J. (2013). *Spark: The Revolutionary New Science of Exercise and the Brain.* Boston, MA: Little, Brown and Company.

Repp, B. H., & Su, Y. H. (2013). Sensorimotor synchronization: A review of recent research (2006–2012). *Psychon. Bull. Rev., 20,* 403–452.

Rosch, K. S., Dirlikov, B., & Mostofsky, S. H. (2013). Increased intrasubject variability in boys with ADHD across tests of motor and cognitive control. *Journal of Abnormal Child Psychology, 41*(3), 485–495.

Sallis, J. F., McKenzie, T. L., Kolody, B., Lewis, M., Marshall, S., & Rosengard, P. (1999). Effects of health-related physical education on academic achievement: Project SPARK. *Research Quarterly for Exercise & Sport, 70,* 127–134.

Sallis, J. F., Prochaska, J. J., Taylor, W. C. (2000). A review of correlates of physical activity of children and adolescents. *Med Sci Sports Exerc, 32*(5), 963–975.

Sibley, B. A., & Etnier, J. L. (2003). The relationship between physical activity and cognition in children: A meta-analysis. *Pediatric Exercise Science, 15,* 243–256.

Schaefer, R., & Overy, K. (2015). Motor responses to a steady beat. *Annals of the New York Academy of Sciences, 1337,* 40–44.

Shape of The Nation Report. (2012). National Association for Sport and Physical Education & American Heart Association.

Shaywitz, S. E., & Shaywitz, B. A. (2008). Paying attention to reading: the neurobiology of reading and dyslexia. *Dev Psychopathol., 20*, 1329–1349.

Shoecraft, Stacey. (2016). *Teaching Through Movement: Setting Up Your Kinesthetic Classroom*. Charleston, South Carolina: Chicken Dance Publishing.

Son, S. H., & Meisels, S. J. (2006). The relationship of young children's motor skills to later reading and math achievement. *Merrill-Palmer Quarterly, 52*, 755–778.

Sowinski, J., and Dalla Bella, S. (2013). Poor synchronization to the beat may result from deficient auditory-motor mapping. *Neuropsychologia, 51*, 1952–1963.

Thaut, M. H., McIntosh, G. C., & Hoemberg, V. (2014). Neurobiological foundations of neurologic music therapy: rhythmic entrainment and the motor system. *Frontiers in Psychology, 5*, 1185.

Thomson, J. M., & Goswami, U. (2008). Rhythmic processing in children with developmental dyslexia: auditory and motor rhythms link to reading and spelling. *J. Physiol. Paris, 102*, 120–129.

Tierney, A., & Kraus, N. (2013). The ability to move to a beat is linked to the consistency of neural responses to sound. *The Journal of Neuroscience, 33*(38): 14981–14988.

Tierney, A., & Kraus, N. (2013). The ability to tap to a beat relates to cognitive, linguistic, and perceptual skills. *Brain Lang, 124*, :225–231.

Tomporowski, P. D. (2003a). Cognitive and behavioral responses to acute exercise in youth: A review. *Pediatric Exercise Science, 15*, 348–359.

Tomporowski, P. D. (2003b). Effects of acute bouts of exercise on cognition. *Acta Psychologica*, 112(3):297-324.

Tomporowski, P. D., Davis, C. L., Miller, P. H., & Naglieri, J. (2008). Exercise and children's intelligence, cognition, and academic achievement. *Educational Psychology Review, 20*, 111–131.

Tomporowski, P. D., Lambourne, K., Okumura, M. S. (2011). Physical activity interventions and children's mental function: An introduction and overview. *Preventive Medicine, 52*, 53–59.

Torgesen, J. K., Alexander, A. W., Wagner, R. K., Rashotte, C. A., Voeller, K. K. S., Conway, T. (2001). Intensive remedial instruction for children with severe reading disabilities immediate and long-term outcomes from two instructional approaches. *J Learn Disabil, 34*, 33–58.

Viholainen, H., Ahonen, T., Lyytinen, P., Cantell, M., Tolvanen, A., & Lyytinen H. (2006). Early motor development and later language and reading skills in children at risk of familial dyslexia. *Developmental Medicine & Child Neurology, 48*(5): 367–373.

Vygotsky, L. S. (1978). *Mind in Society: The Development of Higher Psychological Processes*. Cambridge: Harvard University Press.

Wetter, O. E., Koerner, F., & Schwaninger, A. (2009). Does musical training improve school performance? *Instructional Science: An International Journal of the Learning Sciences, 37*(4), 365–374.

Wrightson, P., McGinn, V., & Gronwall, D. (1995). Mild head injury in preschool children: evidence that it can be associated with a persisting cognitive defect. *Journal of Neurology, Neurosurgery, and Psychiatry, 59*(4), 375–380.

Zervas, Y., Apostolos, D., & Klissouras, V. (1991). Influence of physical exertion on mental performance with reference to training. *Perceptual and Motor Skills, 73*, 1215–1221.

Zelaznik, H. N., & Goffman, L. (2010). Generalized motor abilities and timing behavior in children with specific language impairment. *Journal of Speech, Language, and Hearing Research: JSLHR, 53*(2), 383–393.

Gratitude

Having spent three years writing *70 Play Activities,* I enjoyed much joyful reflection about the mentors, colleagues, patients and family members who inspired, guided and helped me develop the activities that I used in my office, on playgrounds, on tennis courts and even in swimming pools, first as a student and then a pediatric psychologist. Since 1985, I have been developing these activities, yet not one was created on my own. They were all created in spirit or in person within meaningful lasting relationships.

Beginning with my husband and children, who watched me get up at 4:00 am most mornings for three years to write, draw, play and shoot these activities, I thank them, with my most loving heart, for being patient, supportive and caring. I showed them draft after draft, asked them to play activities and even asked their friends to be in a multitude of videos we shot to help clinicians, teachers and children "see" the activities, not simply read about them. Forever I will smile as I picture my husband Rick, the finest therapist I know, watching baseball with one eye and looking at the words and graphics on my iPhone with the other. Rick never said, "Not now, I'm busy," because he knew my heart and soul were in this with a burning passion to reshape how we interact with, educate and help children.

Without my dad, none of this would have been possible, as he has been a supporter of women in business and education for decades.

As neuroscience and cognitive science research has grown to inform education and psychology, my work has become focused on exercise, cognition and executive function. With much gratitude, I feel deep appreciation for the professors, clinicians and colleagues, who took their time to mentor, inspire and guide my professional development. I aim to make a positive contribution to the health and well-being of children to honor them.

Many valued professionals contribute to one's development as a researcher and clinician. From my early years, Dr. Virginia Ford, Dr. Dick Cone, and Dr. John Callaghan, and Dr. Justine Gilman, taught me much about humanity. Knowing them made me a better person. During graduate training, Dr. Ed Shafranske, Dr. Carl Hoppe, Dr. Ron Schouten, Dr. Annette Brodsky, Dr. Karen Saywitz, Dr. Allen Brown, and Dr. Kathy Gilbride emphasized for me, the need to incorporate research in practice. When I was licensed in 1994, I continued to learn and grow in the wisdom of Dr. Raun Melmed, Dr. Gary Perrin, Dr. Paul Beljan, Dr. Laura Wingers, Dr. Alison Reuter, Dr. Koren Ganas and Dr. Ron Fischler. Now, 22 years after licensure, I have been honored with collegial friendships around the world with researchers, scientists and practitioners who dedicate their careers to improving the lives of children. Wendy Young, Nacho Arimany, Dr. David Nowell, Dr. Martin Fletcher, Mary Murray, Dr. J.P. Das, Sue Atkins, Annie Fox, Sue Milano, Dr. Troy Bales, Lauren, Zimet, Dina Beauvais, Paul Rosengard, Ellen Dodge, Dr. Beth Onufrak, Lorraine Allman, Jack Hirose, Laura Hirose, Meg Mickelson-Graf, Stacey Fretheim, Diana Vigil, Dr. Ann Alexander, Jane Lawyer, Dr. Michele Borba, Alex Doman, Deborah McNelis, Dr. Kim Palmiotto, Dr. Gina Madrigrano, Cathy Dees, Abby Dees, Paul Kelly, Dr. Alexandra Brousseau, Maureen Martin, Sheila Allen, Gill Connell, Dana Herzberg, Cheryl McCarthy, Emily Roberts, Jan Katzen, Chris Willhite, Dr. Carol Kenney, Marlaine Cover, Amy Bubier, Shea Schwartz, and Susan Link are just a few of the many friends and colleagues with whom I have had cherished conversations and transformative moments.

Writing a book like this is not an individual effort, it is a community effort involving family, schools, teachers, mentors and researchers. I shared activities with many caring colleagues including Rebecca, who lit the fire that provided me with the energy to complete this book while offering to contribute the activities she uses at the Stanwich School to enhance executive function and social-emotional skills among their students. Rebecca's professionalism, integrity and hard work are incomparable. Even on days when she had a full case-load, as she lovingly parented her four children, anytime I wrote her with a question, she answered within minutes. You are making a meaningful contribution to the field of School Psychology, Rebecca and I look forward enthusiastically to seeing you teach these activities and the ones you create with your students in the future, so that we may empower children to become more involved in the growth of their cognitive, social-emotional, learning and behavioral skills.

Lynne Kenney, PsyD

I am deeply grateful to the people who have taught me and helped me in my professional journey. In my graduate program in School Psychology, at Iona College, Dr. Katherine Zaromatidis was an incredible teacher, role model and supporter. When life impacted my studies, she stood by my side and gave me the time to sort things out so that I could continue to achieve. She may not realize how her encouragement during a difficult time made all the difference and gave me a wonderful idea of what the most compassionate school psychologists could be like. During my internship year, I had talented and professional supervisors who held me to high standards in my work and also took time and care in helping me with their wisdom and guidance. I am thankful to have worked under these two incredible school psychologists, Venessa Green-Davis and Kristin Arita. I am very grateful to my School Psyched Podcast colleagues, Rachael Donnelly, Eric Elias and Anna Smith, in each of whom I confide, question and look to for consultation and collaboration; each is tremendously skilled, knowledgeable and supportive.

I work at an incredible independent school with the most dedicated professional educators to whom I owe an enormous debt of gratitude for their continued collaboration, inspiration, and forward focus in caring for and educating children. The faculty and administration at the Stanwich School in Greenwich, Connecticut are among the finest that I have ever known. It is an honor to work alongside my Stanwich Family, especially my students who are my daily inspiration and motivation to be my best. I am indebted to my dear friend, Katia Scoli, who has listened to me talk about my love for school psychology on endless miles of our long runs together. Katie listens and cares more than any other friend could possible bare to.

To my own family, I could not give my heart and soul to my work if I did not carry the powerful love of my family with me every day. My four beautiful children inspire me to be my best and accept every challenge with courage and hope. Before anything else, I am their proud mother and I am grateful that this love gives me strength and courage. My loving husband, Richard, supports and cares for us with all that he is and is a role model of hard work, dedication and continual personal growth. My list of gratitude includes all the people I am lucky enough to call friends. As Ralph Waldo Emerson wrote, "The glory of friendship is not the outstretched hand, not the kindly smile, nor the joy of companionship; it is the spiritual inspiration that comes to one when you discover that someone else believes in you and is willing to trust you with a friendship." Thank you to my loving friends for believing in me and trusting me with your friendship.

Of course, no list of gratitude would be complete without including my friend and collaborator, Dr. Lynne Kenney. Lynne's passion for supporting children and families is thoroughly contagious and resonant of my own. I am lucky to count her among my mentors and friends; she is kind, talented, skilled and devoted to making a difference.

Lastly, I am eternally grateful for my very first teacher and mentor, my father, Dibyendu Roy Choudhury, a professor turned businessman who never dismissed a question as unimportant and never gave easy answers but instead inspired conversations with patience and love. I have been very blessed to have so much love and support throughout my life.

Rebecca Comizio, MA, MA-Ed, NCSP

Made in United States
Orlando, FL
21 May 2022

18048834R00109